Each in Our Own Tongue

A History of Hispanic United Methodism

Justo L. González

General Editor

Abingdon Press

Nashville

EACH IN OUR OWN TONGUE:
A History of Hispanic United Methodism

Copyright © 1991 by Abingdon Press

Library of Congress Cataloging-in-Publication Data

Each in our own tongue : a history of Hispanics in United Methodism/ Justo L. González, general editor.
   p. cm.
Results of a conference sponsored by the General Commission on Archives and History of The United Methodist Church.
Includes bibliographical references and index.
Contents: Overview/Justo L. González—The South Central Jurisdiction/Joel N. Martínez—The Western Jurisdiction/Félix Gutiérrez—The Southeastern Jurisdiction/Humberto Carrazana—The Northeastern Jurisdiction/Alfredo Cotto-Thorner—The North Central Jurisdiction/Olga G. Tafolla—Puerto Rico/Gildo Sánchez—The next five hundred years/Justo L. González.

ISBN 0-687-11420-9 (alk. paper)

1. Hispanic American Methodists—History. 2. United Methodist Church (U.S.)—Membership. 3. Methodist Church—United States —Membership. I. González, Justo L. II. United Methodist Church (U.S.). General Commission on Archives and History.
BX8247.H57E23   1991
287' .6' 08968—dc20   91-2977

Scripture quotations are from the New Revised Standard Version Bible, copyright © 1989, by the Division of Christian Education of the National Council of the Churches of Christ in the United States of America.

Carlton R. Young

Each in Our Own Tongue

ACKNOWLEDGMENTS

One of the principal needs of The United Methodist Church has been to recover and make known the history of its racial/ethnic membership.

During the fall of 1984 and the winter of 1985 the General Commission on Archives and History of The United Methodist Church sponsored a series of four two-day consultations. This event brought together historians and leaders from United Methodism's Asian American, Black, Hispanic and Native American communities. Each of these consultations reviewed and assessed what had been done regarding the history of its constituency and what needed to be done to recover its story. This volume, one of a series of four, is the result. We are confident that it makes a significant contribution to our denomination's history.

The General Commission on Archives and History is grateful to the General Conference, and especially to the General Council on Ministries, for the financial support which has made this and the other volumes possible. We also express our appreciation to the authors and editors whose expert labors now broaden our knowledge of the history of the church, and to the United Methodist Publishing House without whose cooperation there would be no series. A special word of appreciation goes to Rebecca Marnhout who skillfully copy edited all four volumes.

Present and former members of the General Commission's staff, Carolyn DeSwarte Gifford, Susan M. Eltscher, and C. Jarrett Gray, Jr. have made important contributions to this project.

MAJOR J. JONES, *Chairperson (1980–1988),*
Ethnic Heritage and History Committee

CHARLES YRIGOYEN, JR., *General Secretary,*
General Commission on Archives and History

How is it that we hear, *each of us, in our own native language?* Parthians, Medes, Elamites, and residents of Mesopotamia, Judea and Cappadocia, Pontus and Asia, Phrygia and Pamphylia, Egypt and the parts of Libya belonging to Cyrene, and visitors from Rome, both Jews and proselytes, Cretans and Arabs—in our own languages we hear them speaking about God's deeds of power.

Acts 2:8-11

¿Cómo, pues, les oímos nosotros hablar *cada uno en nuestra lengua* en la que hemos nacido? Partos, medos, elamitas, y los que habitamos en Mesopotamia, en Judea, en Capadocia, en el Ponto y en Asia, en Frigia y Panfilia, en Egipto y en las regiones de Africa más allá de Cirene, y romanos aquí residentes, tanto judíos como prosélitos, cretenses y árabes, les oímos hablar en nuestras lenguas las maravillas de Dios.

Hechos 2:8-11

CONTENTS

PREFACE

As this book is being sent to press, all of us who have been working on it have a very clear sense that the task has only begun. Its publication is an invitation to others to join in the task of recovering a history that lies hidden, in more ways than one. This is not the history we hear when we attend large United Methodist bicentennial celebrations. Nor is it the story we hear in classes on American church history or in books on the history of Methodism.

To correct that standard reading of history by calling attention to often-forgotten chapters is much more than an intellectual task, or one we undertake for reasons of antiquarian curiosity. Indeed, Hispanic United Methodists, like many other minorities in our culture, find our very existence denied and marginalized, not only by structures of power and authority that bypass us but also by a telling of history that bypasses us. As the history of the church is envisioned and taught in most United Methodist circles, there is a progressive narrowing of the people whose history is studied—and in that narrowing process many of us are left out. When dealing with late antiquity and the early Middle Ages, the history of the expansion of Christianity into Great Britain, Germany, and Scandinavia is studied, but the parallel history in Spain is ignored. Later, when considering the great intellectual awakening of the twelfth and thirteenth centuries, attention is focused on the Crusades and their impact and on the universities of Paris and

Oxford, but little or nothing is said of the importance of pilgrimages to Santiago, of the Spanish Reconquista, or of the interpreters of Toledo, without whom the renaissance of the twelfth century would have been inconceivable. When we come to the sixteenth century, all attention is centered on northern Europe and the Protestant Reformation, and church historians often forget that at the same time that the Reformation was taking place in northern Europe, the conquest was taking place in what is now Latin America (and that it is still too early to tell which of these two events will be of greater significance for the history of the church). At this point in our studies, we United Methodists tend to forget about most of Europe (except for a heavy dose of intellectual interest in nineteenth-century German theology) and concentrate on events in England. From England we cross the Atlantic with Wesley and Oglethorpe and Coke and Asbury.

In that entire process, we Hispanics are left out. We have no history. And having no history, we have no identity in The United Methodist Church. We are made to feel as if we do not really belong in it. Thus to those among our United Methodist brothers and sisters who are constantly calling for greater evangelistic zeal and asking why our membership is declining, we say that the recovery of our United Methodist Hispanic history is a contribution, no matter how small, to the evangelistic task of the church, for such recovery will tell Hispanics that they do indeed have a place and a home in The United Methodist Church.

The task, however, is not easy. Precisely because our history has been denied for so long, many among our own people have little interest in the history of Methodism. History is something that those in the church from the dominant culture have, and we do not. History will only serve to underscore our recent arrival in this communion, and thus to further disempower us. Thus it is rare to find Hispanic United Methodists with an interest in the history of the denomination, or even in the history of Hispanics within the denomination.

This is not to say that we do not have an interest in our own history. Many congregations have appointed their own historians, who with little or no training or guidance try to chronicle events they consider significant in the life of their faith community. Many celebrate anniversaries in which that history is retold and relived. Many church members zealously guard old records, photographs, and other such material.

What exists, then, is not disinterest but distrust. People are not willing to give up such materials and place them in archives basically because they are not convinced that the agencies of the church at large will value them and care for them. This, which is true of some segment in any of our constituency, is true to a greater degree than usual among Hispanics. Our people wish to keep their own records, or at least to keep them in places that have shown a genuine appreciation for them.

Needless to say, this has caused and continues to cause the permanent loss of many irreplaceable records. And this is one of the reasons why we feel that the task has only begun. What lies ahead is the difficult task of establishing mutual trust and support between our own Hispanic constituency and those whose task it is to help us preserve the priceless documents of our inheritance. It is our hope that this book, published as it is under the auspices of the General Commission on Archives and History, will be a contribution in that direction.

Then, there is another sense in which this small volume is only a beginning. There is much to be done by way of interpretation, even of the materials included here. Much of what the reader will find in the pages that follow is a chronicle of events, leaders, structures, organizations, and so on. It is necessary to know this in order to take any further steps. Yet it is those further steps that will make this history most meaningful and significant as we plan our future. The further steps that are still necessary have to do with critical analysis. While in the pages that follow there are some hints at that analysis, such hints are not systematized or substantiated in a critical way.

For our purpose, this critical analysis must take at least two directions, which must be kept in constant dialogue and tension. The first is the theological dimension: What were and are the theological presuppositions of mission among Hispanics? What were and are the theological stances of Hispanics themselves in their efforts to carry forth their own mission? Related subjects include the vision of Hispanic culture and the tradition of Hispanic Methodists, the attitudes of the dominant culture toward Hispanic realities and their vision of the goal of society (such as melting pot, integration, segregation, and other theories), the manner in which the dominant culture in general and the United Methodist tradition in particular have looked at the traditional Roman Catholicism of Hispanics, and so forth.

A second set of issues, closely related to the first, has to do with social, political, and economic analysis. Among what classes in the Hispanic community has Methodism made inroads? Why? What have been the social, political, and economic agendas, both of Anglos and of Hispanics, in the entire process? How have policies toward Hispanics been affected by policies toward other minorities? How did the structures of The United Methodist Church and of its predecessor denominations affect or determine the socioeconomic profile of Hispanic Methodism? These two sets of questions, while distinct, must not be kept apart from each other, for it is clear that theological presuppositions will affect social and political agendas, and vice versa.

While this analysis is done, however, history will continue, for history never waits for historians, nor for any of its other participants. It is important for us to remember that, for our task is ultimately not one of curiosity but one of obedience. The question is not simply what happened or how and why it happened. The question is, in light of what happened, and of our best understanding of it, what is our responsibility and our mission? Thus we launch this book with a mixture both of humility for its many shortcomings and of gratitude to the Lord who, even in the midst of our shortcomings, calls us to ever-greater and ever-renewed obedience.

CONTRIBUTORS

The Reverend Joel Nefatalí Martínez, author of the chapter on the South Central Jurisdiction, is a native of Seguín, Texas, and an ordained minister of the Río Grande Conference. After completing his studies at the University of Texas at El Paso and at Perkins School of Theology, he served pastorates in Dallas, San Antonio, and El Paso. From 1975 to 1981 he served as a staffmember of the National Division of the General Board of Global Ministries. Upon his return to Texas, he was appointed to serve as district superintendent of the Northern District, Río Grande Conference, a position he held until 1987. During part of that time (1984–88) he also chaired the Missional Priority Coordinating Committee of The United Methodist Church. He currently serves as pastor of Emanu-El United Methodist Church in Dallas, Texas. He is married to Raquel Mora Martínez, and they have three children. Mr. Martínez is a founding member of the National Hispanic Caucus (MARCHA) and is currently its national president.

Félix Gutiérrez, Ph.D., is a professor in the School of Journalism at the University of Southern California, a member of the South Pasadena United Methodist Church, and a former member of the General Commission on Communications. He is the grandson of the Reverend Esaú P. Muñoz, a Methodist minister who served Spanish-speaking churches in Mexico, Texas, Arizona, and California from 1912 to 1950. He thanks his

15

mother, Rebecca Muñoz Gutiérrez, his uncle, Rosalio Muñoz, and his aunts, Elizabeth Grijalva and Josephine Rodríguez, for helping him during his research for the chapter on the Western Jurisdiction.

Dr. Humberto P. Carrazana is a retired minister in the New York Annual Conference who served also in the Annual Conferences of Cuba and Florida for a total of forty-four years as a pastor, district superintendent, principal of several schools, and university professor. He is a graduate of Candler College and of the Seminario Metodista, both in Cuba, and holds an Ed.D. from the University of Havana. He served for two four-year terms as president of the board of trustees of the Evangelical Theological Seminary in Matanzas, Cuba, and for three quadrennia chaired the Board of the Ministry of Cuba. He was editor of the *Revista Trimestral*, forerunner of the present *Lecciones cristianas*. He is a frequent contributor to various church publications and currently resides in Miami.

The Reverend Alfredo Cotto-Thorner, who has contributed the chapter on the Northeastern Jurisdiction, is a retired minister of the New York Annual Conference, where he served as pastor of the South Third Street United Methodist Church, in Brooklyn, from 1949 to 1988. He received his theological education at Eastern Baptist Theological Seminary. In 1960, while a pastor in Brooklyn, he founded Anchor House, a residential rehabilitation center for drug addicts and alcoholics. In 1972 and again in 1980, he represented his Annual Conference as a delegate to General Conference. He also was a member of the steering committee of MARCHA from 1975 to 1980.

Ms. Olga G. Tafolla, author of the chapter on the North Central Jurisdiction, is a lifelong member of the Methodist (and then The United Methodist) Church, where she has been active at every level. As a member of the organization of United Methodist Women, she has served in many capacities, from local circle leader to conference president in 1984–88. She has been assistant dean and the dean of the Midwest Regional School of Christian Mission. She has been a delegate to Jurisdictional Conference three times and to General Conference twice. For eight years she was a director of the General Board of Global Ministries, serving in the National Division and in a number of committees of the board. Presently she serves as a consultant for the Women's Division Program on Undesignated Giving and as Director of the General Council of Ministries. She lives in Battle Creek, Michigan, with her husband, Lott E. Tafolla. Her two daughters are married and live in other states.

The Reverend Gildo Sánchez, who has contributed the chapter on Puerto Rico, is a retired church executive, educator, and pastor who currently serves as Mission Interpreter for the General Board of Global Ministries. He received an S.T.B. degree from the Evangelical Seminary of Puerto Rico in 1945 and an S.T.M. degree from Union Theological Seminary in New York in 1951. He has served as field representative for church extension and as professor and president of the Evangelical Seminary of Puerto Rico (which granted him the D.D. degree in 1985). Active in the ecumenical movement, he was present at the First Assembly of the World Council of Churches in Amsterdam, in 1948. He and his wife, Angélica, have a son, Jorge, who is a pastor in northern New Jersey, and a daughter, Alba, who is a librarian at the University of Puerto Rico.

Justo L. González, author of the opening and closing chapters of this book and its general editor, is a ministerial member of the Río Grande Conference. Born in Cuba of parents who were both ordained Methodist ministers, he studied at the Evangelical Theological Seminary in Matanzas, Cuba, and then at Yale University, where he received the S.T.M., M.A., and Ph.D. degrees. In 1961 he joined the faculty of the Evangelical Seminary of Puerto Rico, where he also served briefly as its dean. In 1969 he moved to Decatur, Georgia, in order to teach at Candler School of Theology, where he served until 1977. Since that time, while still living in Decatur, he has devoted all his energies to research, writing, and the development of Hispanic leadership in several denominations. He is the author of over forty books and a number of articles, as well as editor of *Apuntes*, a journal of Hispanic theology. He is currently director of the Hispanic Summer Seminary Program of the Fund for Theological Education.

The typing of both the English and Spanish versions of this volume, as well as much of the necessary correspondence, has been the responsibility of Mr. Javier Quiñones-Ortiz.

1

OVERVIEW

Justo L. González

A LONG HISTORY

To tell the history of Hispanics and their relation to The United Methodist Church, beginning at the time of the first converts to Methodism, would be to begin the story at the middle. Indeed, Hispanics have a long history in what is now the United States, and also a history that touches that of United Methodism at more than one point.

In a way, Hispanics date their origins to that great encounter between two races, two traditions, and two worlds that took place beginning on October 12, 1492. It was an awesome encounter—a mighty clash, but not a meeting. One civilization overswept another; one race enslaved another; one history submerged another, but those who had the power to conquer the others did little to understand and appreciate them. In spite of all the glorious tales, it is not a pretty story. It is a story of prejudice, plunder, and rape. On one side, it was a story of valiant resistance weakened by petty division and ancient superstition. On the other, it was a story of gross injustice propelled by Christian arrogance and its own form of superstition. And, to compound crime with further crime, soon another stream of humanity was added to our tragic history, as enslaved black humanity flowed in from Africa, to fill the pockets of the wealthy and to impoverish their souls.

It is from that history that we have sprung, and it is that history that still lives in us. We are the children of conquistadors and Indians, of slaves and masters. We have experienced in ourselves, and from both sides of the equation, what pride of race and culture and creed can do. Even today, as we struggle to keep our culture in order to keep our identity, we know that our own culture carries in itself the memory of a thousand oppressions—those committed by our ancestors against others, those committed by others against our ancestors, and those committed by our ancestors against one another.

That history has deep roots in what is now the United States. Indeed, in the United States only the Native Americans have a longer history. Long before the Mayflower compact, and long before the founding of the major cities of the Northeast, Hispanics had founded cities in Florida and the Southwest and had crisscrossed the continent. Of those days the memory still remains, not only among Hispanics but also in the very names of several states of the Union: Florida, so named after Easter, the feast of "Pascua Florida"; California, the land of heat; Nevada, the land of snow; Colorado, the red land; New Mexico. And it remains also in a thousand names of cities, mountains, and rivers: San Francisco, Los Angeles, San Antonio, Santa Cruz, Sacramento, Río Grande, Sierra Nevada, Grand Teton . . . Today, many Hispanics may be immigrants or the descendants of relatively recent immigrants, yet the fact remains that even these immigrants have not come to an entirely alien land, but to a land where their culture has deep roots. It is necessary to remember this if one is to understand the readiness with which Mexicans cross a border that they still remember as a human creation, or the surprising persistence of the Spanish language even among those whose ancestors have lived under the American flag for generations.

The Wesleyan tradition also touches on Hispanic history in the remote past, long before the existence of The United Methodist Church—or even of the Methodist Church and the Evangelical United Brethren. John Wesley began studying Spanish in 1736, mostly in order to communicate with the Indian population of Georgia, many of whom had learned Spanish from Jesuit and Franciscan missionaries. Governor Oglethorpe would not allow him to carry forth this enterprise, and Wesley used his Spanish to read the Spanish mystics. He had high regard for some of them—including quietist teacher Miguel de Molinos—and one wonders how much these readings, at the very time when he was going through his spiritual quest just before Aldersgate, influenced his later theology and piety.

As Methodism began its worldwide missionary expansion, it touched the Hispanic population again and again. One must remember that some of the earliest Methodist missionaries went to the Caribbean, the one point in the world where interaction between British and Spanish traditions was most constant, and one may surmise that as Methodism grew in the British Caribbean, it must have come into contact with Hispanics. Also, at the same time as Methodism was taking its first steps among the Hispanic population in the United States, it was making a concerted missionary effort in Latin America. It is important to remember this, for as we shall see repeatedly in the chapters that follow, there has been a constant and growing connection between Hispanic Methodists in the United States and their brothers and sisters in Latin America.

Finally, one must remember that Hispanics who become United Methodists come to their new faith community with a long tradition of Christianity deeply embedded in their culture. For centuries, Hispanic social life has revolved around Christian ceremonies and celebrations such as baptisms, weddings, saints' days, funerals, and the like. The religious expressions of Hispanics may be different from the expectations of the dominant culture, but nevertheless they are expressions of centuries of Christian influence on Hispanic culture. Two examples should suffice: First, there is the entire institution of *compadrazgo*—a word that cannot be translated but that means something like "co-parentage." What this means is that the persons who stand as godparents for a child in baptism acquire an obligation toward that child and its family that is parallel to that of the child's natural parents. *Compadres*— co-fathers—and *comadres*—co-mothers—play an important role in some Hispanic traditions. This institution, a puzzlement to many an outside observer, is a testimony to the importance

21

Mexicans and others grant to baptism, so that one has relatives not only by blood but also by baptism. Second, it is instructive to look at Christmas traditions in Hispanic culture. Among Hispanics, gifts are brought by either the Christ Child or the Three Kings. Santa Claus, reindeer, and Christmas trees are relatively recent imports. Thus while Protestant Anglos claim that *they* follow biblical faith and practice and that Hispanic Catholics have departed from the biblical faith, the latter could very well ask, where in the Bible do you find Santa Claus, reindeer, and Christmas trees?

Thus although many a Hispanic sees in conversion to Protestantism (or more specifically to Methodism) a break with the past, that break is not usually as radical as we believe. No matter how radical that conversion may be, it must be seen as a significant landmark in a history that is already centuries old, and on which the new Methodist reality is built. It is important for us to realize this, for otherwise we would not be placing the chapters that follow in their proper context.

WHAT'S IN A NAME

As we embark on the study of the history of Hispanic Methodism, it is important that we realize who are these people called "Hispanics," some of whom are also part of "the people called Methodist."

First of all, there is the question of how to call us. On that subject there is no unanimity. Some object that the word "Hispanic" overemphasizes our Spanish heritage, to the detriment of our Indian, black, and in a number of cases even Oriental heritage. One alternative is "Latino," and this is preferred by some. On the other hand, there are also objections raised against such a designation. For one thing, it too harkens to our European roots, shortchanging the others. For another, even the name "Latin America," now generally accepted, was originally a designation made current by the French, who sought to use their "Latinity" as an advantage in the struggle with Great Britain to gain hegemony over the area. Others among us, in an effort to emphasize the mixture of races and traditions that stands at the very heart of our being, prefer to refer to ourselves as *Raza*—"Race," with a capital *R*—meaning that we are the race that is no race but a mixture and combination of all.

Then various subgroups among those whom we generally call Hispanics and Latinos also call themselves in various ways, each with a slightly different emphasis; for example, there is a subtle but important difference of opinion among those who prefer to call themselves "Mexicans," those who prefer "Mexican Americans," and still others who speak of themselves as "Chicanos."

In conclusion, all names, if taken too literally, are insufficient. "Hispanic" and "Latino," as used in the chapters that follow, are descriptions that must not be taken strictly in their original etymological sense but as shorthand to include the Hispanic-Indian-Black-Oriental-generally-Spanish-speaking people that we are. Likewise, the designation "Anglo," often used to refer to the dominant culture in this society, should not be taken to imply that all "Anglos" are genetically descendants of the ancient Angles. It too is shorthand for the British-German-Scandinavian-French-and-others-English-speaking-whites who constitute and shape the dominant culture in our society.

SOME STATISTICS

No matter what we call ourselves, a few demographic data may be in order so that the reader may know the nature and size of the population to which we are referring. The census of 1980 counted 14.6 million Hispanics in the United States, plus another 3.2 million in Puerto Rico. All are agreed that this is an undercount, for large numbers of Hispanics were not included in the census. Thus even at the time of the census, estimates of total Hispanic population in the United States and Puerto Rico ranged between 19 and 25 million. In any case, even leaving aside those who were not counted, the figures of 1980 represent a very significant increase, for they mean that in 1980 Hispanics were 6.4 percent of the total population, as compared with 4.5 percent ten years earlier.

The Census Bureau also issued a series of projections with a number of variables. The lowest projection was that by the year 2080 there would be 30.6 million Hispanics in the United States, or 17.6 percent of the total population. The highest projection foresaw a staggering 140.74 million by the same date, or 27.9 percent of the total population. In 1988 the Census Bureau issued an approximate count of Hispanics that seems to indicate that of all these projections, the highest is the most likely.

In sharp contrast to commonly held notions, 71 percent of all Hispanics in the United States (or at least, of those counted by the census) are native U.S. citizens. In Texas, 81 percent of all Hispanics are native citizens. Thus in spite of all the public discussion and debate regarding immigration, the greatest continuing source of population growth among Hispanics is fertility. The census of 1980 reported this growth at 3 percent per year. In order to understand the significance of this figure, one may compare it to the present rate of growth among the population at large (0.9 percent) or to the rate during the much-discussed Baby Boom (1.9 percent).

It is also significant that even though most Hispanics have been born in the United States, the vast majority also continue to speak Spanish. According to the census of 1980, one-eighth (12.5 percent) of all Hispanics spoke only English, an equal number were bilingual but preferred English, and the rest either spoke only Spanish (19 percent) or were bilingual with Spanish preference (56 percent).

Bilingualism, however, has been seen as a hindrance rather than an advantage by the educational establishment, which is mostly monolingual. In very few settings are bilingual students encouraged to make use of their language skills for academic purposes. This, combined with a high poverty index, has resulted in an enormous gap between the academic attainments of Hispanics and those of the general population. One of every four Mexican Americans and Puerto Ricans in the United States is two or more years behind in school. Fifty-eight percent of all

Hispanics finish high school (compared with 88 percent for the rest of the population). Fewer than 10 percent have college degrees, compared with almost 25% for the total population. The current policy of emphasizing private funding for education and cutting back on federal supports has not helped Hispanics. Indeed, between 1978 and 1983, while the level of support from private institutions to white college students rose by 15.6 percent, the parallel figure for Hispanic students dropped by 4.5 percent.

Parallel statistics indicate that the poverty rate among Hispanics is also exceedingly high, having risen from just under 22 percent in 1979 to a steady 29 percent to 30 percent during most of the 1980s. In 1985 39.9 percent of all Hispanic children were poor. And the situation is not improving, for between 1986 and 1987, while the median income for white families rose by 1.1 percent, that of Hispanic families dropped by 2 percent.

These statistics, sad as they are, do not provide an adequate picture of the level of poverty among Hispanics. For one thing, they refer only to those whom the census counted, and it is clear that a high proportion among the uncounted—migrant and other farmworkers, undocumented aliens, and so on—are among the poorest of Hispanics. For another, the poverty line is determined by a ratio between income and number of members in a family. This is applied within the framework of the nuclear family that the dominant culture considers normative. Hispanics, in contrast, still keep the tradition of the extended family, and therefore many who live in the United States send a significant portion of their income to relatives abroad whom they consider their dependents but whom neither the Census Bureau nor the Internal Revenue Service count as such. If these extra obligations were taken into account, the poverty rate among Hispanics would be much higher.

DIVERSITY

There are several subgroups among Hispanics. Of these, the most numerous is the Mexican American, with almost 9 million members according to the census of 1980. Their greatest concentrations are in California (3.6 million) and Texas (2.8 million), with large numbers in every state of the Southwest. In recent years, they have been moving to other states, especially in the Midwest. Illinois, whose Mexican American population was relatively small in 1970, now has well over half a million.

The dominant facts in the history of Mexican Americans, after the Spanish conquest, are the Mexican-American War and its prelude, the annexation of Texas by the United States. As a result of those events, more than half of what had formerly been Mexican territory became part of the United States—the states of Texas, New Mexico, California, Nevada, Utah, and part of Colorado. Since there was Mexican population on both sides of the resulting border, crossing back and forth continued unabated and practically unhindered for years.

At first, the flow of population was mostly southward, as Mexicans who had been engulfed by the advancing United States decided to move south of the border, often complaining that the stipulations of the Treaty of Guadalupe-Hidalgo protecting their rights and properties were not fulfilled. Then, as cheap labor was needed for the development of the American Southwest, the flow was reversed, and large numbers of Mexicans began crossing the border into the United States in order to work here. There have been a number of attempts to regulate that flow, such as the *bracero* program of the 1940s and 1950s and the more recent immigration law. However, studies show that the main factor determining the number of people who cross the border is not its patrolling or the laws that seek to control it but the relative economic and political conditions on both sides of the border. During the Mexican Revolution, large numbers crossed into the United States. During the Depression, 400,000 were deported, including many who were native U.S. citizens. Then, when Mexico was riding the wave of high oil prices, immigration decreased drastically, only to reach new heights after the collapse of the Mexican economy in the 1980s.

The second largest group of Hispanics is the Puerto Ricans, of whom the census counted over 2 million in 1980 (plus the 3.2

26

million on the island). They have traditionally settled in the Northeast, particularly in and around New York City. The census of 1980 reported that almost two-thirds of all Puerto Ricans in the United States lived in the states of New York and New Jersey, with significant numbers in Connecticut, Massachusetts, Pennsylvania, and even as far as Illinois, Florida, and California.

The dominant fact in the history of the Puerto Rican population is the Spanish-American War of 1898, which resulted in Puerto Rico's becoming a possession of the United States. The economic and social changes that this brought about were enormous. In 1899 Puerto Rican farmers and peasants owned 93 percent of the productive land. By the 1930s 60 percent of sugar production on the island was controlled by four large American corporations, and foreign investors controlled 80 percent of tobacco production as well as the totality of maritime commerce. In the 1950s and 1960s "Operation Bootstrap" brought economic prosperity by giving tax and other incentives to American investors and by concentrating on light industry rather than agriculture. By 1985 only 1.7 percent of the gross economic product of Puerto Rico was derived from agriculture, and food had to be imported both from the mainland and from the Dominican Republic. By that time, evolving economic conditions throughout the world had brought about a near collapse of much of Puerto Rican light industry, and the island was going through very hard times. Less than half of the population was economically active, and unemployment rose to more than 20 percent.

In that context, the dominant political issue in Puerto Rico has long been the question of status. Should Puerto Rico seek to become a state of the Union? Should it become an independent republic? Should it keep its present status as a Commonwealth (*Estado Libre Asociado*) under the American flag and Constitution? Should that status evolve into something else? Such are the questions that have dominated the political scene in Puerto Rico for decades and that are constantly impinging on the life of the church on the island as it makes decisions regarding its own message, organization, and relations with the rest of the denomination.

As in the case of Mexico, migration between the United States and Puerto Rico is controlled primarily by economic factors. During the postwar years, and before Operation Bootstrap came into full swing, migration to the mainland accelerated rapidly. Then, as Operation Bootstrap increased economic opportunities on the island, migration decreased and at a point even reversed, with more Puerto Ricans returning to the island than migrating to the mainland. Finally, as recession set in again, migration to the United States increased once more.

At present approximately half of all Puerto Ricans living in the United States were born there. Many live in poverty. In 1982 the median family income of the Puerto Rican population in the United States was $11,148, less than half that of the population at large ($23,907). For years, unemployment has remained at two to three percentage points above the national average—double the national average in the case of Puerto Rican women.

The third largest subgroup among Hispanics is the Cubans. In 1980 they numbered 803,226, or 5.5 percent of the Hispanic population. While there are significant numbers of Cubans in New York, California, New Jersey, and other states, their largest concentration is in Florida.

The dominant fact in Cuban immigration is the Revolution of 1959, which produced several waves of exiles. Until 1980 these exiles tended to come from the higher and best-educated classes in Cuba, and therefore Cuban immigrants have not generally faced the conditions of continued poverty of other Hispanic groups (although their median family income is normally about 75 percent of that of the rest of the population). In 1980 the Mariel boatlift brought an additional 125,000 Cubans to Florida. These were generally less skilled and educated than the earlier arrivals and have since experienced conditions similar to those of other Hispanic immigrants.

Even before the Revolution of 1959, however, there was a significant Cuban colony in Florida. Many of these were exiles or the descendants of exiles who had left Cuba during the period of Spanish domination or had fled one of several dictatorships that arose after independence. As we shall see, this community of early immigrants played an important role in the history of Hispanic United Methodism in the region.

Finally, in the census of 1980 more than 3 million Hispanics classified themselves as "other Hispanics." This is roughly one-fifth of all Hispanics. These include large numbers of Central Americans, Dominicans, and Colombians. Probably the figure also includes many of the descendants of the Mexican inhabitants of the Southwest before the war with Mexico, who often refer to themselves as "Hispanos," in contrast to the "Mexicanos" who have arrived later.

The differences among these various groups are important. Traditional foods vary greatly. Some eat tacos, others eat *arroz con Gandules,* and still others eat *congrís.* Some have tortillas, others don't. Some douse their food with hot red peppers, others reach for the garlic and olive oil. The same is true with music: Mariachis, rumba, and salsa are all Hispanic, but they are not the same. The inflections of the language vary, and Hispanics joke among themselves about how the members of some other group "sing" when they speak.

Yet there is also a unity among the various groups. In our last chapter we shall have opportunity to mention some of the signs of that unity among United Methodist Hispanics. Here, however, it may be well to point out that even the census data, while not seeking such information, point toward that unity. Indeed, if one follows the patterns of migration within the United States of each of the three main groups, one sees that they tend to go where other Hispanics are already settled. Thus the main concentrations of Cubans outside of Florida are in New York, New Jersey, and California, all states with large Hispanic populations. Puerto Ricans, when they move beyond the Northeast, go to Illinois—a state with a rapidly growing Mexican American population—or to California, Florida, and Texas. And the fastest growth of the Mexican American population outside the West and Southwest is in Illinois, Florida, and several northeastern states. In short, Hispanic population follows other Hispanic groups. This both reflects the commonality that already exists and produces new commonalities. Thus a new Hispanic consciousness is arising that goes beyond regionalisms or subgroups and that will be an important factor in the political, social, cultural and religious life of the United States.

COMMON TRENDS IN OUR UNITED METHODIST HISTORY

Before moving on to the following chapters, which outline the history of Hispanic United Methodism by regions, it may be well to highlight some of the common characteristics, trends, and issues that appear in several of those chapters.

One characteristic of Hispanic United Methodism that will become apparent in the pages that follow is that its strength is in direct proportion to its connection with centers of Hispanic culture outside of the United States. Although this point should be obvious, it is necessary to underscore it, for it has significant implications for the future planning and structure of Hispanic work. Such work in the Northeast draws much of its strength from its constant connection with Puerto Rico and, in more recent times, with the Dominican Republic. On reading the chapter on that jurisdiction, the reader will note that a large percentage of the pastoral leadership of Hispanic churches in the area comes from Puerto Rico and the Dominican Republic. At an earlier time, there were also a number of Cuban pastors in the area. There is constant coming and going between New York and Puerto Rico, and that constant traffic strengthens the church at both ends. Likewise, Hispanic churches in the West and Southwest also draw much strength from the traffic across the border with Mexico. And although such traffic is now interrupted, much of the Hispanic work in Florida has evolved out of the connections between Florida and Cuba.

At some stages during its development, Hispanic work in various areas has been organized to take this into account. For instance, the Southwest Spanish Mission of the Methodist Episcopal Church included not only New Mexico, Colorado, and parts of Arizona and Texas but also the Mexican states of Sonora and Chihuahua. At a slightly later date, the Northwest Mexico Mission Conference of the Methodist Episcopal Church, South, reached beyond its center in the Mexican states of Chihuahua, Sonora, and Durango to include a church in Phoenix, Arizona. In what is presently the South Central Jurisdiction, the Mexican Border Conference of the Methodist Episcopal Church, South, had two districts in Texas and two in Mexico. In Florida, early in the twentieth century, the Cuban-Spanish Mission and its successor, the Florida Latin District, included both appointments within the state of Florida and missionary appointments to Cuba. In the Northeast the traditional contact between that region and Puerto Rico is signified in that the Puerto Rico Annual Conference is part of the Northeastern Jurisdiction—although, for less defensible reasons, until recently it has been attached to the Philadelphia episcopal area.

While the value of these contacts is acknowledged by such de facto arrangements, they have not usually been incorporated into the total strategy for work among Hispanics by The United Methodist Church or by the denominations that gave it birth. Traditionally these denominations—like the present United Methodist Church—divided their missionary concerns between domestic and foreign concerns, as is seen currently in the existence of the National and World divisions of the Board of Global Ministries of the United Methodists. Work in Latin America— except in Puerto Rico—is part of the latter, while work among Hispanics in the United States is part of the former. The result is that the national missionary structures are not calculated to enhance the give and take between U.S. Hispanics and their sisters and brothers from across the border, from whom U.S. Hispanics draw much of their inspiration and strength. Although at times there have been efforts to overcome this situation, the very structure of the missionary agencies of the church has not been calculated for their success. Also, when the domestic mission among Hispanics has been lodged in foreign missions departments, as was the case with the work of the Methodist Episcopal Church, South, in Texas until 1914, the emphasis has usually been on the foreign side of the mission, with the result that work among Hispanics within the United States has suffered.

This leads to another issue that is a central concern of the Hispanic United Methodist constituency. That is the issue of identity versus assimilation. In the pages that follow, the reader will find that this issue appears at various levels. It is a question families and individuals have to face, as new generations arise whose rootage in the Hispanic tradition may not be as deep as that of their ancestors. Children who grow up watching television in English, attending schools that teach in English, and generally being part of the dominant culture in the United States will clearly have difficulties relating to the earlier generations in their own families whose upbringing was different. Thus in the Hispanic community the generation gap is often also a cultural gap. Families and individuals have to face this issue not only in terms of their cultural and language preferences but also in terms of the economic and social structures in which they live. Very few, if any, try to dissuade the younger generation from learning English. Where conflicts sometimes arise is in the insistence of the older generation that their children should also know Spanish and be rooted in Hispanic culture. Bombarded by cultural images and symbols that persuade them that Spanish and the culture it represents are second class, many in the younger generation resent their parents' insistence on their traditional culture. Thus one often finds families in which one generation speaks only Spanish, the next generation is bilingual, and the third speaks only English or is bilingual with a strong English preference. Still, one should not exaggerate this transition, for according to the census, although 71 percent of all Hispanics are U.S. citizens by birth, 75 percent are bilingual with Spanish preference, or speak only Spanish.

This poses an important problem for local churches. On the one hand, since the church is one of the few culture-setting environments the older generation can control, they often see it as a place where their children can learn and practice not only the Christian faith and values but also the language and culture of their ancestors. Needless to say, among the young this often causes resentment toward the church, or feelings that as they outgrow their elders' attachment to Hispanic culture, they will also outgrow their need for the church. On the other hand, there are many Hispanic churches that follow the opposite tack, having either bilingual services or two separate services, one in each language, and holding Sunday school classes in Spanish for adults and in English for children and youth. This solution, however, also presents difficulties, for most of the churches that follow this policy are set in barrios where there are still large numbers of new immigrants whose children do not know English, and therefore this policy implies that the church will be concerned primarily with its own children and lose much of its appeal to the more recent arrivals. Also, there is now among many in the younger generation a quest for identity, a search for their cultural rootage in the language and traditions of their ancestors, and many of these younger people hope to find support for their quest in the Hispanic church. Thus there are no easy solutions, and the question of assimilation versus identity has remained a crucial one throughout the history of the Hispanic church.

It is, however, at the level of church structures that this question will appear most frequently in the pages that follow. The various denominations that merged to form The United Methodist Church have wavered in their policy on this matter. There have been times when it was felt that Hispanics should have their own ecclesiastical structures, and times when it was felt that such structures should be dissolved and the Hispanic church should be assimilated into the rest of the connection. It will also be clear from the pages that follow that very seldom have Hispanics themselves had a voice in deciding these matters. In the chapter on the Western Jurisdiction, for instance, one can read of the disappointment of the Hispanic constituency when the Latin American Provisional Annual Conference was assimilated into the California-Arizona Annual Conference. In Florida, at the time of the merger of 1939, the Latin District was dissolved and incorporated into the various geographical districts of the Florida Conference. In the Northeast, one reads of the desire to have a full-time coordinator of Hispanic work in the New York

Conference, and of disappointment at not having such a coordinator. Significantly, in every case in which Hispanic structures have been dissolved or integrated into larger structures, church growth among Hispanics has declined. One should also note that the production of Hispanic leadership—especially pastoral leadership—has been in direct proportion to the existence of ecclesiastical structures for Hispanic self-determination.

A third issue that should be clear in the pages that follow is that The United Methodist Church and the denominations that preceded it have not had a strategy for Hispanic work. This was true at the beginning and has been true throughout most of our history. In the beginning, Hispanic churches generally resulted from the interest of an Anglo congregation or its pastor, or from the missionary work of a Hispanic convert. At most, such Hispanic work was able to arouse the interest of a district or an Annual Conference, and it was only after it was well established that the general agencies of the church took part in its support. This should not be seen only in negative terms, for mission is always most effective at the local level, and excessive planning "from above" is seldom conducive to relevant mission. Yet the lack of planning and coordination also carried with it lack of reflection as to the particular circumstances of Hispanic work. Thus, for instance, we read of regional missionary structures for work with Hispanics, Portuguese, and Italians. While there are many cultural commonalities among these three groups, there is one important difference these structures failed to take into account: the difference between crossing the border and crossing the Atlantic. As a result, while the Portuguese and Italian communities tended to assimilate into the wider population as new generations arose, the Hispanic community had a permanent identity that the leaders of the mission did not take into account. When it came to mission among Hispanics, the work was often based on untested and unspoken assumptions that seldom came to the foreground, precisely because there was little national or regional planning and therefore little reflection on the nature of such work.

This lack of planning and reflection has led to another characteristic of Hispanic work that will be seen in the chapters that follow. There has been little consideration of the manner in which Methodist structures and policies affect Hispanic work, and no effort made to adjust such structures and policies in order to respond to the needs of mission among Hispanics.

As an example of how this has affected the total work of the church among Hispanics, one may take the issue of the economic level of most of the Hispanic community, and the difficulties Methodist policies and structures create in such a situation. As the census and other statistical data show, a significant portion of the Hispanic community lives below the poverty line, with many others barely above it. Yet this is seldom taken into consideration in planning for mission among Hispanics.

This affects Hispanic work in a number of ways, all related to the middle-class status of the majority of the United Methodist constituency and the unspoken expectation that most United Methodists will belong to the same class. Thus when new Hispanic work is begun in a community, it is expected as a matter of course that it will eventually become self-supporting. If that is not achieved after a reasonable time of subsidized mission, the work is considered a failure. It is closed down, and the church looks for a different and more promising field in which to invest its missionary resources. At the same time, the requirements that a newly established congregation must meet in order to be considered "successful" and self-supporting are set by outside expectations, and these expectations arise out of a generally middle-class church. In his chapter on the Northeastern Jurisdiction, the Reverend Alfredo Cotto-Thorner indicates that for a congregation in his Conference this means a budget of $40,000 a year for salary and administrative expenses alone, plus whatever expenses are necessary for the purchase and maintenance of facilities, and so forth. Similar figures apply in other areas. Such expectations can only be met by middle-class churches or by very large churches in poor areas. This means that by definition most United Methodist work in the poorer barrios, which is where the majority of the Hispanic population lives, is programmed for failure. This is even more so since such outside expectations tend to overpower and eventually destroy the new congregation's own sense of stewardship for mission. If no matter how much a congregation engages in sacrificial giving—and many Hispanic churches do—most of their resources must go toward meeting expectations set by others, and very little result is seen in the fulfillment of the mission at the local level, congregations soon lose their enthusiasm for giving, and even for the mission. After a number of years of subsidized existence, with very little growth either in numbers or in giving, the work in the barrio is declared to be a failure and closed down. The net result is that a denomination that has correctly and justly fought against red-lining by banks ends up unwittingly practicing its own form of red-lining and establishing congregations only in those areas where churches can become self-supporting by middle-class standards.

A related matter, and one that appears in several of the chapters that follow, is the issue of the sharing of physical facilities with another congregation, or of receiving the full use of buildings already in existence. This is a common practice, and the manner in which most Hispanic work is started (except in the two Hispanic Annual Conferences of Río Grande and Puerto Rico). At first glance this is a very sensible arrangement. The church has a number of buildings that are being underused, often in areas with high Hispanic population. What better use could be devised for these facilities than to make them available for newly formed Hispanic congregations, or for Hispanic groups within existing congregations? Again, this would be a very good policy if it were accompanied by the necessary reflection and analysis, so that strategies could be planned that take into account the realities of the communities involved. This, however, is not the case. As will be seen in the chapters that follow—particularly in those on the Western, Northeastern, and Southeastern jurisdictions—the sharing of buildings, or simply passing them on to Hispanic congregations, has taken place without much thought being given to anything but the most immediate considerations. A neighborhood is in transition. A building that was originally built for a large and flourishing church is now too large for the dwindling congregation. Those who were most disturbed by the racial change in the neighborhood have already left both the neighborhood and the church. Those who remain are a combination of the elderly who cannot or will not move, those whose antiracist convictions impel them to stay, and the die-hards who will not let "those other people" take over. They have an increasingly hard time meeting their budget, and the maintenance of their building facilities is an important part of that budget. The leaders of the church at the district and conference levels are concerned that sooner or later it will be necessary either to close down that church and sell its property or to begin subsidizing it. Either course would be difficult to justify. At the same time there is a growing Hispanic community around the church—or even a newly formed congregation meeting in someone's living room. The solution is obvious. Make the facilities of the dwindling church available for Hispanic work. If it is necessary to subsidize it, there should be little objection to this, for this is a subsidy not to an old and dying congregation but to a newly established mission effort. Hispanics are happy at receiving the use of such excellent facilities; the older congregation is happy at seeing its building better employed, especially if this also involves a lessening of their financial burden; and the administrative levels of the district and conference are relieved at having found a solution to a problem. Yet more often than not, the solution is not really such. Many in the older congregation begin to transfer their grief over the changes in the church to the newly arrived Hispanics, who are soon made to feel as unwelcome or at best tolerated tenants. The Hispanic congregation grows increasingly discouraged at having most of the financial resources they can muster be invested in the upkeep of a building that is not their own, and not in program and missionary outreach. Eventually, the "solution" fails, and the Hispanics are made to feel as if it is their fault.

A further theme that will appear in the pages that follow is that the jurisdictional structures of The United Methodist Church—and of the former Methodist Church—have made it very difficult for Hispanics in various areas of the country to attain a measure of unity and a vision of their common mission. This is aggravated by the fact that Hispanics in various jurisdictions tend to be mostly members of one of the various subgroups of Hispanic population—Puerto Ricans in the Northeast, Cubans in the Southeast, and Mexicans in the West and the South Central area. Thus to the traditional differences among these various groups has been added the distance created by the boundaries among various jurisdictions. As a result, it was only in recent years, as we shall see in other sections of this book, that a national Hispanic United Methodist consciousness has been arising. Signs of this are the national Hispanic caucus, MARCHA, and the election, after many years of struggle, of the first Hispanic bishop—by the Western Jurisdiction in 1984. The matter of episcopal elections is a prime example of the manner in which the jurisdictional structure has hampered self-determination among Hispanics. There are two Spanish-speaking Annual Conferences in the connection, and there are significant numbers of Hispanics in every jurisdiction. Yet the very existence of jurisdictions, and the role these play in episcopal elections, has meant that Hispanics have not been able to support one another, and that neither of the two Spanish-speaking annual conferences has ever been headed by a Hispanic bishop.

These observations, however, are not the whole story. They are not even the central fact of our story. They are a backdrop without which our history cannot be understood; but they must remain the backdrop and not usurp the center of the stage. At the center stands the undeniable fact that we exist because it is the will of God, expressed and sealed by the action of the Holy Spirit, that we hear the gospel "each in our own tongue." It was in the power of the Spirit that the first Hispanics embraced Methodism, and it is by the power of the Holy Spirit that we have survived and even increased in the face of circumstances, policies, and structures that have not always been favorable. It is the Spirit who unites us with other sisters and brothers who do not speak our language or share in our traditions but who also hear and celebrate the same faith, each in their own tongue. And it is the Spirit who repeatedly gives testimony within our spirits, in our own tongue, that we too are beloved children of God.

2

THE SOUTH CENTRAL JURISDICTION

Joel N. Martínez

The emergence of Hispanic Methodism in the Southwest is a part of the vigorous expansion of Protestant Christianity in the nineteenth century. It was occasioned by the encounter of two peoples, two nations, and two cultures in the region now commonly referred to as the Borderlands. This region included what are now the states of Texas, New Mexico, Arizona, Colorado, and California.

This encounter was the result of the United States' drive for territorial expansion toward the Pacific Ocean. It was perceived by many in the United States as a divinely inspired "manifest destiny" to extend U.S. cultural values throughout the North American continent. Mexico, however, with its newly acquired independence from Spain, perceived it as a march toward empire at Mexico's expense. Through armed conflicts in Texas during 1835–36 and the war with Mexico of 1846–48, the United States achieved what much of the U.S. press and most pulpits proclaimed as the fulfillment of the divine will. Through the annexation of Texas in 1845 and the Treaty of Guadalupe-Hidalgo in 1848, the United States acquired over half of Mexico's territory.

The encounter between United States and Mexican peoples was within the dynamic of the conqueror and the conquered. It is only by taking into account this context of conflict, war, and eventual domination that one can attempt an adequate interpretation of the present reality of the church in the Southwest, including The United Methodist Church.

The history of Hispanic United Methodism in the area can be divided into five periods as follows: the beginnings (1821–85), the period of missionary structures and administration (1885–14), the critical years (1914–39), the years of revitalization and growth (1939–68), and the period of self-determination and the end of isolation (1968 to the present).

THE BEGINNINGS (1821–85)

It was the challenges and demands of new situations that brought two men onto center stage in the beginnings of Methodist history among the Spanish-speaking peoples of the Southwest. Benigno Cárdenas and Alejo Hernández lived through personal and communal crises that would bring them to an encounter with the gospel and would draw them into a new history with their Lord. The two crises they experienced were the Mexican-American War of 1848 and the French invasion of Mexico in 1862.

For Cárdenas the war of 1846–48, concluded by the Treaty of Guadalupe-Hidalgo on February 2, 1848, represented an unwelcome change in cultural, political, and religious terms. As a Mexican priest in Santa Fe, New Mexico, Cárdenas was suddenly placed under the supervision of a French-born bishop in an Anglo-dominated society within the bounds of a different nation. Cárdenas and other priests in Santa Fe and northern New Mexico resisted the new order of things. To understand this resistance, one must take due account of the reality of a neglected Roman Catholic constituency in northern New Mexico, the strong nationalistic feelings of Mexicans against the French, and the independent spirit of priests serving on the far frontiers of the diocese of Durango, fifteen hundred miles distant.

On his return from a trip to Rome to protest against his bishop's actions, Cárdenas made a stop in London. There he visited with Methodist missionary William Rule. Rule had served for a time in

Spain. He encouraged Cárdenas to consider working as a missionary for the Methodists and gave him a letter of recommendation. Cárdenas then visited the Missionary Society of the Methodist Episcopal Church in New York City. Those same days the society was considering sending the Reverend Enoch C. Nicholson as a missionary to New Mexico. The society invited Cárdenas to join Nicholson and work as a missionary to the Spanish-speaking population of New Mexico. Cárdenas accepted.

Upon their arrival in Santa Fe in November 1853, Nicholson and Cárdenas sought opportunity for Cárdenas to announce publicly his new affiliation with the Methodists. Having been denied a hall in which to hold services, they determined to hold an open air preaching service in the plaza. There, in front of the governor's palace on November 20, 1853, Cárdenas preached the first sermon in Spanish by a Methodist in the Southwest. The Methodists welcomed Cárdenas, his gifts, and his experience into their ministry. He was therefore able to continue with his vocation among the people to whom he had originally been called.

Rome had adjudicated in Cárdenas's favor, and one can only surmise what motivated him to leave the Roman Catholic Church. Was it revenge against his bishop? Was it fear of retribution by the bishop? Was it a change in his theological perspective? Was it his strong nationalistic feeling directed against the new order of things? All of these? We do not know for sure. What is not in question is that Cárdenas, through his preaching and teaching, helped lay the foundation for the later mission to the Spanish-speaking residents of New Mexico.

In the case of Alejo Hernández, the French invasion of Mexico in 1862 was the moment of his first step toward his eventual service as a Methodist minister. Alejo was in seminary at Aguascalientes, Mexico, studying for the priesthood, when he joined Benito Juárez's army of resistance. He, along with many other faithful Catholics, resented the Roman Catholic hierarchy's blessing of the invasion. Hernández, while on duty as a soldier, happened on a book entitled *Nights with the Romanists*. This was an anti–Roman Catholic tract left by another soldier, a member of the U.S. army, during the 1846–48 war with Mexico. Hernández,

41

his curiosity awakened by many references to the Bible, sought a copy of the Holy Scriptures. He made his way to Brownsville, Texas, in search of the Bible. While there, he underwent a deep religious experience in a small English-speaking church and began his ministry of witnessing. He describes his experience in Brownsville:

I was seated where I could see the congregation but few could see me. I felt that God's spirit was there, although I could not understand a word that was being said. I felt my heart strangely warmed. . . . Never did I hear an organ play so sweetly, never did human voices sound so lovely to me, never did people look so beautiful as on that occasion. I went away weeping for joy. (Náñez, 1981, p. 43)

He was eventually to become the first Mexican ordained to the Methodist ministry. His short years of service (1871–75) included organizing the first Methodist congregation in Mexico at Mexico City in 1873. Ironically, Hernández sailed from New Orleans in 1873 for the port of Veracruz. He landed at the same port where eleven years earlier, in 1862, the invading French army had landed. Now Hernández came with the Word of one who brings down the mighty, raises up the weak, and gives hope to both. He was later ordained elder in Mexico City in 1874. So he is recognized as father to Methodism in both Texas and Mexico.

As is often the case, the mission of the church among the Mexicans and Mexican Americans of the Southwest grew from the vision of faithful individuals rather than the strategy of a church body. The efforts of laity, in particular the work of Sunday school teacher William Headen in Corpus Christi and the Bible distribution by David Ayers in the Galveston area, were part of the larger missionary movement of the period. Many great mission movements begin with a devoted individual who eventually draws a whole church into mission.

This was also true in New Mexico, where Ambrosio González sustained a Bible study group from 1855 to 1869 without clergy or mission board support. González had been the first convert in 1854. It was on the good foundation of such work that Thomas Harwood would reopen the New Mexico mission in 1869. As is often the case, the mandated structures and agencies follow rather than lead, respond rather than initiate.

Thomas Harwood, to his credit, recognized that indigenous clergy and laity would be the key factor in the mission to Spanish-speaking people. At the same time, he did urge the Anglo ministers to prepare for ministry in Spanish. In fact, he called on the seminaries to teach Spanish as part of their course of study! (Náñez, 1981, p.17). Bishop John C. Keener, another early participant in the development of ministry to the Mexican Americans, commented in an article written in 1878, "Methodism has been completely Mexicanized!" (Náñez, 1981, p.55). This statement points to an early recognition that the church needed to take root in such a way that leadership would emerge from that planting. Many years would pass, however, before missionaries would understand and affirm the role of indigenous leadership at every level of church life.

Indeed, the prevailing attitudes of the Anglos to the defeated Mexicans living in their midst was such that it is a wonder much success in mission resulted. The feeling Mexicans had toward Anglos can be traced to the treatment summarized by Bishop James O. Andrews in a visit to Texas in 1843: "But the extreme wickedness and irreverence of the American soldiery and the many early immigrants who settled among them, have rendered our access to them doubly difficult" (Náñez, 1981, p. 40). One can understand why such a history would inevitably hinder the message and work of mission in the years ahead.

In summary, the events leading to the encounter of the Mexicans of the Southwest with the Methodist Church were war, conquest, and the annexation of Mexican territory by the United States. In the midst of those turbulent times, some experienced the transforming power of the gospel. They responded, in their own context, to service in the ministry of Christ. They brought new cultural gifts and accents into the life and language of Methodism. They were to draw the Methodist movement more deeply into the Hispanic reality, thereby expanding the meaning of the Wesleyan vision of a world parish.

MISSIONARY STRUCTURES AND ADMINISTRATION (1885–1914)

The period from 1885 to the time of the Mexican revolution (1910–14) was characterized by the appearance of the first missionary units devoted to ministry to Spanish-speaking people in both Texas and New Mexico. In New Mexico, the superintendent of the New Mexico mission, Thomas Harwood, asked the General Conference of the Methodist Episcopal Church to create a separate mission to serve Hispanics, due to the growing numbers of members and churches. This was granted, and the participants in the new mission gathered at Peralta, New Mexico, in September 1885.

This new mission, the New Mexico Spanish-Speaking Mission, was to last until 1892. It was succeeded by the New Mexico Mission Conference, which continued until 1907. In the period 1885–1907, the growth in its extent and membership was impressive: It began with two districts and grew to five, and it grew from 410 members to 3,117. The extent of the territory covered in 1907 is indicated by the locations of district offices: Albuquerque, Santa Fe, Las Vegas, all in New Mexico, and the El Paso and Sonora districts in Texas and Mexico.

Parallel to this development was the organizing of the Mexican Border Conference of the Methodist Episcopal Church, South, at San Antonio, Texas, in October 1885. Until then, the ministry among Mexican Americans was lodged in two mission districts, one headquartered in San Diego (near Corpus Christi), the other in San Antonio. The West Texas Conference had initially created a Mexican border district in 1874. Previous to this, Alejo Hernández, after being ordained at the 1871 Annual Conference session at Leesburg, Texas, was sent to Laredo as his first appointment. The request for the creation of a Conference to serve the expanding ministry to Hispanics was first voted by the West Texas Conference in 1878. This request to the General Conference was finally approved in 1882. The new Mexican Border Conference had four districts, two headquartered in

Mexico (Monterrey, Nuevo León, and Monclova, Coahuila) and two in Texas (San Antonio and El Paso).

These mission units were under the leadership of missionaries. The only Mexican Americans with any administrative roles were the Reverend Santiago Tafolla and the Reverend Alejandro de León, who served as presiding elders for the San Antonio and Monclova districts, respectively. Of course, the superintendents of the Conferences were missionaries. Thomas Harwood was to lead the New Mexico Mission from 1885 to 1907. Alexander Sutherland was to serve in the same capacity in the Mexican Border Conference until 1893. This was to be the prevailing pattern of missionary administration until recent times.

The delayed recognition and affirmation of indigenous leaders in the Southwest by the mission structures retarded the full indigenization of the church. This tendency, not at all unique to the Methodists, was in later decades a principal driving force moving the Mexican Methodist Church toward autonomy. The church in Mexico, parenthetically, became the first of the Methodist family in Latin America to achieve autonomy, in 1930.

From the beginning until 1914, the administration of mission in the Southwest and in northern Mexico was lodged in foreign missions departments. This was an indication that efforts in Mexico were to receive priority. This was evidenced by the greater number of social, educational, and welfare centers and programs established south of the border.

The placement of mission and ministry with Spanish-speaking people in units that included both sides of the border had positive and negative consequences. Dr. Náñez believed that the tendency to focus on Mexico was to affect the development of a strong Methodist Hispanic church in the Southwest. Commenting on immigration to the United States during the Mexican Revolution, he stated: "This sudden influx posed a serious problem to the Methodist Church which had been serving the Spanish-speaking community. The work in the United States had been neglected, so there were not enough churches or ministers to serve the newcomers" (Náñez, 1981, p. 63).

Another negative consequence was the perpetration of the

notion that Mexican American citizens residing in the southwest United States were foreigners, and foreigners are not entitled to the full rights and privileges of the rest of the citizenry. The result of this arrangement in missionary administration was to further delay the full participation of U.S. Hispanics in United Methodism's structures, institutions, and ministries.

The tides of Mexican immigration had ebbed more than flowed since 1848. This changed with the Mexican Revolution, which began in 1910. This, the first social revolution of the twentieth century, was to displace millions of people and unsettle Mexican life for a generation. Many crossed the Río Grande during the decade of 1910–20. Statistics were not kept since there was an open border between Mexico and the United States. Although some returned, a sizable number stayed. This first significant immigration wave presented the border states and their institutions, including the church, with a new situation. Just at this time, the Methodist Church was ill-prepared to minister to the new immigrants. Most of the church's strength in congregational, educational, and social service programs was in Mexico, not Texas or New Mexico. Therefore, the capacity to respond was limited at a time when the need was great.

With the increasing difficulty brought on by unstable social and economic conditions in Mexico, the Board of Missions of the Methodist Episcopal Church, South, decided to establish a separate administration for the mission in Texas. At a meeting in Laredo on February 10–11, 1914, the Mission Board officers and missionaries working in the Border Conference determined to place the mission work in Texas under the domestic missions unit. The new unit in Texas was to be known as the Texas Mexican Mission. This recommendation went to the General Conference later that year and was adopted.

Since all Mexican leadership was excluded from the missionaries' meeting in February 1914, the Mexican pastors had a separate meeting. They wanted the Methodist Church, South, to commit itself to an Annual Conference structure because they feared the consequences of being "integrated" into the English-language Conferences. Although the General Conference did not grant the request for Annual Conference status, this petition signaled the seriousness with which the indigenous leadership was to treat the matter of merger later on.

Meanwhile, in New Mexico, the New Mexico Mission began to decline rapidly. From five districts in 1907, the mission was left with one district by 1914. Further change came in 1915 when the remaining district in the mission was reduced to the status of a district in the English-speaking mission.

The decline in New Mexico occurred primarily as a result of administrative changes. The changes in administration created uncertainty and instability. This was to be the pattern of New Mexico Hispanic Methodism in future decades. Decision making by mission board officials and missionaries with no input from the indigenous leadership would lead to discouragement and decline.

During this time women were crucial in teaching, organizing, and financial support roles in the mission to Hispanics. The early sponsors of social service centers, clinics, and schools were the women's missionary societies in both the northern and southern branches of the church. These groups would supply not only funds but also personnel to lead in the meeting of educational, health, and sociocultural needs of persons served by the Methodist Church in the Southwest, as well as in Mexico. The deaconess movement was to supply many leaders for the schools, centers, and clinics that served the needs of the poor, especially children and women. Schools like the Holding Institute in Laredo, Effie Eddington in El Paso, the Harwood Girls' School in Albuquerque, and the Valley Institute in Pharr were staffed in their early years primarily by deaconesses. The contribution of these women as leaders and workers in the mission with Mexican Americans in the Southwest represents one of the better moments in the history of mission service.

The emphasis on education and educational institutions was an important feature of the mission work of Methodism from the beginning. From Thomas Harwood's opening of a school at Cherry Valley in a renovated chicken coop in 1870 to the establishment of the Lydia Patterson Institute in El Paso in 1913 and the Mexican Methodist Institute in San Antonio in 1917, the educational effort was an integral part of the mission. It is noteworthy that the Methodist Mission in New Mexico was credited with modeling the future development of the public school system for the state of New Mexico.

These Methodist schools and institutes served as crucial centers of leadership development for the Methodist Hispanic Church in Texas and New Mexico. Lydia Patterson Institute and the Mexican Methodist Institute (later Wesleyan Institute), for instance, served as the basic source of clergy training for nearly thirty years. The Holding Institute and Harwood School were especially successful in providing several generations of laity with good secondary school preparation. Although some of these schools no longer exist, the Río Grande Conference remembers their vital contribution.

In summary, the period 1885–1914 was that time when the challenge of mission to the Spanish-speaking people of the Southwest began to find institutional expressions in Methodist structures and programs. During this period, decision making and control were firmly in the hands of missionary administrators, with minimal input from the indigenous leadership. And throughout this period, priority mission efforts were directed toward Mexico rather than the southwest United States.

In the watershed decade of 1910–20, Spanish-speaking Methodism in Texas was granted a new opportunity with the creation of the Texas Mexican Mission at Austin, Texas, in November 1914. The promise of a strengthened ministry was being seized with increasing hope. At the same time, a once-flourishing New Mexico Mission was in serious decline. These contrasting situations were to become more evident at the merger in 1939.

THE CRITICAL YEARS (1914–39)

This would be a period of difficulty for Mexican Americans in the Southwest and for the church as well. During these years, anti-Mexican attitudes would deepen in the United States. The

48

raid of Pancho Villa on Columbus, New Mexico, in 1916 would fan resentment against all Mexicans, citizens or not. During World War I the courting of Mexico by Germany, most especially the promises of restoration of land to Mexico if she joined Germany's cause in the war against the United States, served to fuel anti-Mexican feelings. Finally, during this period the Great Depression would ravage the economic landscape of the United States. As a response, the U.S. government would forcibly expel hundreds of thousands of Mexicans.

The sizable immigration occasioned by the Mexican Revolution of 1910–17 continued during World War I (1917–18) as the need for labor increased. However, deportation was to occur during 1920–21 as the need for agricultural workers decreased. This pattern was to follow in 1930–35 during the height of the Depression.

During the 1920s, U.S. immigration policy began to change. In 1924 the Border Patrol was established. In 1925 legislation was introduced in Congress seeking to place Mexico under the quota system for legal immigration. Although this legislation failed, it occasioned the testimony of nativistic and racist groups in support of the proposed restrictions. The successors to these groups have continued to this day. But it was the economic misery of the Depression in the 1930s that would produce the worst of the attitudes toward Mexican immigrants. By some estimates, close to half a million or more people were deported during the 1930s. The largest number of these were from Texas. The message was clear: Mexican labor is tolerable when economic conditions warrant it; Mexican people are unwelcome when their sturdy backs and dexterous hands are no longer needed.

The years 1914–39 were a time of transition coupled with the demands for new structures. In Texas the struggle would include persistent demands for an Annual Conference. In New Mexico the pattern of structural changes or rearrangements would continue to diminish the church's effectiveness.

In Texas, the establishment of the Texas Mexican Mission in 1914 did not dim the dream many had of a full Annual Conference. The 1929 Annual Conference session voted to request the 1930 General Conference to grant the Texas Mexican Mission status as an Annual Conference. Citing growth in numbers, finances, and trained leadership, the request was strongly supported. The General Conference granted the request. On October 16, 1930, the Texas Mexican Conference was born in Brownsville, Texas. Twenty-seven pastors were transferred from membership in the Border Mexican Conference into the new Conference. All the time from 1914 to 1930, pastors serving in the Texas Mexican Mission had had to keep their membership in Mexico. The new Conference reported (in 1931) 3,837 members and a Sunday school enrollment of 3,814. The Conference was to have two districts: the Valley District, with Frank Ramos as presiding elder, and the Northern District, with Dr. Frank Onderdonk, the former superintendent of the Texas Mexican Mission, as presiding elder.

Meanwhile, in New Mexico, "From 1914 to 1939, the work seemed to be without direction, and the different structural changes that were tried, more than efforts to save the situation, were momentary decisions made with the hope that the problem would go away" (Náñez, 1981, p. 29). A listing of the structural changes from 1915 to 1936 gives fuller meaning to this observation:

1915 New Mexico Spanish Mission becomes a district in the New Mexico Mission.
1923 The Southwest Spanish Mission is organized (includes churches in Kansas, Colorado, and Arizona, as well as New Mexico).
1931 New Mexico Spanish churches become part of the Latin American Mission, based in California.
1936 The Spanish churches again become part of the English-speaking mission in New Mexico.

The word "survival" is an apt description for the ministry of Spanish-speaking churches in New Mexico during this period. Methodism did not serve the Spanish-speaking people of New Mexico with the excellence and promise that characterized its beginnings under Benigno Cárdenas, Ambrosio González, and Thomas Harwood.

Leadership Changes

The Texas Mexican Conference witnessed two important changes in leadership during the decade of the 1930s. One change occurred at the death of the Reverend Frank Onderdonk in 1936. A former general superintendent of the Texas Mexican Mission, Onderdonk was presiding elder of the Northern District in San Antonio. At his death, the presiding bishop, Hiram A. Boaz, seriously considered replacing Dr. Onderdonk with another missionary. This prospect was opposed by the Reverend Alfredo Náñez and others. They saw the need for elimination of double standards in compensation and status. Missionaries employed by the Board of Missions were paid different salaries and were accountable to the Board. More important, Náñez and others felt it was time for Mexican Americans to assume more leadership in the ministry to their people. After careful reflection, and with the urging of Mexican American leaders, the bishop named Frank Ramos to replace Dr. Onderdonk. With this appointment, the administration of the Texas Mexican Conference was now under the guidance of a leader drawn from among the people.

The second change was the entry of women into the pastoral ministry. Toward the end of the 1920s, Elodia Guerra, a lay preacher, had been named by Frank Onderdonk as Conference evangelist. She preached with zeal and eloquence throughout the Conference. Later, in the early 1930s, two other women began their ministry as lay preachers: Carolina Farias in Mission and Dolores Arévalo in San Antonio. These women were the pioneers of women in the ordained ministry in the Río Grande Conference.

In spite of economic scarcity, discrimination, and neglect, ministry with Spanish-speaking people survived. In New Mexico the decline continued until merger in 1939. A series of structural moves aided rather than prevented the decline. In Texas there were foundations being laid for a future period of growth and vitality.

YEARS OF REVITALIZATION AND GROWTH
(1939–68)

The merger of the three separate streams of Methodism in 1939 also united the Hispanic Methodist streams in New Mexico and Texas. The legislated unity would be difficult to realize in practice.

New Mexico's people were descendants of families resident in the area since Spanish colonial days (prior to 1821). They did not understand themselves as Mexican but as Spanish. In Texas, on the other hand, most people were first- or second-generation residents. The greatest concentrations, near the border, maintained close familial and cultural ties to Mexico. The Spanish language was spoken differently in the two areas. In addition, the geography would make it difficult to develop new contacts and relationships. It is seven hundred miles from Albuquerque to San Antonio and nearly a thousand miles from Albuquerque to the lower Río Grande Valley. Beyond all this, the church experience had been different. In New Mexico, the ministry with Spanish-speaking people had been in decline since the peak year of 1907. That year over 3,100 members were reported. At the time of merger in 1939, fewer than 500 members and four ministers joined the new Conference. In Texas the church had experienced steady, if not spectacular, growth.

Undoubtedly, the size of the groups coming into merger made inevitable the feeling in the smaller that they would be absorbed by the larger. All of these differences were to be exacerbated when the name chosen for the new Conference included the word "Mexican" in it. The Southwest Mexican Conference was to carry that name from 1939 to 1948. At the 1947 Annual Conference session, it was voted to request a change of name. During the Jurisdictional Conference, the committee considering the request recommended the name Río Grande Conference. This was adopted and well received by all in the Annual Conference. This change was a major factor in easing tensions, especially on the part of the people in New Mexico.

The new Conference was organized on November 3, 1939, at Trinity Methodist Church in Dallas. The membership of the new unit included 6,364 full members and 6,682 enrolled in Sunday school. It consisted of three districts: the western, the northern, and the southern. It included all of Texas and New Mexico and overlapped six of the English-speaking Conferences. Dr. Alfredo Náñez summarized three basic challenges facing the new Conference: its enormous geographic expanse, the diversity and complexity of its constituency, and the organizational requirements to function effectively as an Annual Conference.

Another continuing challenge was addressed early in the new Conference's life. The academic requirements for entering the Spanish-speaking ministry had always been lower than those for other ministers. The new Conference, in one of its first actions, asked the 1940 General Conference to eliminate this special provision. The leadership preparing for Hispanic ministry would abide by the same requirements as everyone else. This was adopted by the General Conference. This action symbolized that Hispanics wanted to be full participants, *con dignidad,* in the life of the church.

The decade of 1940–50 was to be the most effective in terms of church growth. An increase in membership of 52 percent (3,388) represented a faster growth rate than the Mexican American population growth rate in Texas and New Mexico during the same time. Dr. Náñez does not credit planning or methodology but a "spirit of revival" for the dramatic growth (1981, p. 99). It is noteworthy that in 1946 the Conference led the denomination in percentage of membership growth. And during the initial phase of the Crusade for Christ in 1946, the Conference was the leader in proportionate giving to the Crusade (Nail, 1958, p. 124).

On the local level, the Annual Conference grew in its financial support as well. At merger in 1939, only four charges were self-supporting. By 1950 the number had risen to nineteen. Likewise significant was the establishment of a Conference Pension Program in 1943. Although meager in its compensation, it represented the first regularized program for the Hispanic ordained ministry. The priority of pensions had been low for the missionary leadership since they were assured their pensions through the Board of Missions.

All these statistical measures and reports reflect a vigor and vitality seldom matched in United Methodism. The current Conference leaders would do well to reexamine this period for lessons in the ministry of evangelization.

The Conference also experienced a new era in the growth of leaders among laity. Vital contributions to the church's ministry were made by the groups discussed below: women, youth, young adults, and men. The most energetic and mission-conscious lay group in the Río Grande Conference has always been the women's organization. The forerunners of United Methodist Women organized into a Conference unit in November 1933 in San Antonio. This group was known as the Woman's Missionary Society. It became the Women's Society of Christian Service (WSCS) after the merger in 1939. The Wesleyan Service Guild, primarily for women working outside the home, also was organized in 1970. Finally, after 1968, the WSCS became United Methodist Women.

In 1944 the Mission Program materials were first translated into Spanish for use by Spanish-speaking women's groups throughout the church. The translator was a lifelong Río Grande leader, Mrs. Elida G. Falcón. That same year, for the first time, a Río Grande woman, Mrs. Minerva N. Garza, attended a Jurisdictional School of Missions. Later in 1964 Mrs. Clotilde F. Náñez would become the first Hispanic woman to serve on the General Board of Missions. This kind of leadership was a strength in the life of the Conference at all levels, especially the local.

The far-seeing Conference WSCS established a Ministerial Scholarship Fund at their meeting in 1941. This fund predated an effort by the Conference men's organization for a similar purpose. The WSCS ministerial scholarships would be vital in the preparation of ministers well into the 1960s.

The participation of women in the life and ministry of Hispanic Methodism was always wholehearted but was rarely accorded the richly deserved recognition that was its due. It is time to recover and retell the story of the contributions by women to the mission and ministry of the Hispanic church.

The Conference youth group had been organized in the former

Texas Mexican Conference during 1933 at an assembly at Holding Institute. Josué González, later a distinguished minister and Conference leader, was the first president. The Conference Youth Organization grew so rapidly that its annual meeting was moved to the Methodist camp at Kerrville. This location was more geographically central to the new Conference.

The vigorous life of the youth organization had three important results, according to Dr. Náñez (1981, p. 101). First, the youth ministry in local churches was nurtured and revitalized. Second, many young persons responded to the call to ministry in these highly motivated assemblies. Third, and probably most critical, the organization was a leadership development laboratory. A strong sense of solidarity through shared experiences was to help overcome the previous generation's differences, noted earlier. Mount Wesley in Kerrville would become a unifying and invigorating experience for many who were to lead the Conference as adults.

In 1941 the young adults formed a Conference-level organization at Mount Wesley in Kerrville. By the beginning of the 1950s, the young adult organization and program in the Río Grande Conference was judged a model for the denomination. Mr. Alfredo Vásquez, a young adult leader from San Antonio, was to travel in Latin America and Europe interpreting the efforts realized by Hispanic young adults in the church.

A unique experiment with young adults from three Conferences happened in the early 1950s. It included the Río Grande Conference (Hispanic), the West Texas Conference (black), and the Southwest Texas Conference (Anglo). Through joint planning and leadership, the young adult constituency of these three Conferences opened up a new future in a time of social and cultural segregation. This model would later be repeated among youth of the three Conferences in the 1960s.

The laymen of the Conference also developed a Conference-wide organization during this period. The emphasis of the laymen was on stewardship education and the promotion of financial support for ministry. Mr. Juan Uranga and later Pete Zepeda would provide outstanding leadership to laymen of the Conference. This happened primarily through the Conference Board of Lay Activities.

One outstanding project the men developed was the sponsoring of a scholarship program. This program continues to the present day. The WSCS discontinued its program when the men initiated theirs. The scholarships are not limited to ministerial students, although these have priority.

This period in the Conference's history would witness a shift in the center of theological training from Lydia Patterson Institute to Perkins School of Theology at Southern Methodist University (SMU). Prior to the 1940s, only one graduate of SMU served in the Río Grande Conference, Alfredo Náñez. All other ministers had been trained at the Wesleyan Institute in San Antonio or Lydia Patterson in El Paso, or in Latin America. The action of 1940 eliminating exceptions in academic requirements signaled the beginning of a new attitude toward theological preparation. The younger clergy were encouraged to study for their baccalaureate and continue their education in seminary. By 1950 seven additional Hispanic students had entered Perkins School of Theology. This number was to double in the 1960s.

A related development was the initiation of the Conference Course of Study School in Spanish in 1951 at SMU. Prior to this, these courses were offered at Lydia Patterson or by correspondence. The establishment of Spanish-language course work at SMU was a belated recognition by the General Board of Education and the seminary of their responsibility to the Hispanic church. The impetus came from the Río Grande Conference as it sought to upgrade the education of its ministerial leadership. Drs. Ben O. Hill and Alfredo Náñez were the key leaders in this effort.

As noted earlier, the Río Grande Conference had always been sensitive about double standards. It sought full participation in the denomination. A determined effort to eliminate parallel tracks between missionaries and indigenous leaders in terms of compensation and status had occurred in 1936. But the tendency to ignore Hispanic input in decisions affecting the Hispanic church reappeared in 1949. In that year, the General Board of Missions created the position of Director for Spanish and Indian

Work. The office was located in San Antonio. The intent of the office was to promote support for the ministry with these groups in Texas, New Mexico, and Oklahoma. A large part of the effort was devoted to raising monies through the Advance Program. The job description, however, was written without consulting with Hispanic leaders, and it did not clarify the relationship between the Office and the Conference. The end result was years of tension, misunderstanding, and mistrust between Conference leadership and the Office of the Director.

The key issue was administrative authority. The Office of the Director, often without consultation with district superintendents and other Conference officers, unilaterally made or withheld grants to churches, to the detriment of the Conference and its authority. This was to continue until 1964, when the National Division of the Board of Missions redefined the role of its office in San Antonio.

This chapter in the life of the Annual Conference reminded many that vigilant involvement in general agency policy making was ever more necessary. It also gave the Conference a deeper understanding of the discriminatory practices and policies of earlier periods.

The decade of the 1960s was to usher in some hard issues and questions for the Conference. A central one was intensified by the government's efforts on behalf of the poor. Would the many churches located in the poorest barrios become involved in enabling the war against poverty, or would they avoid it?

With students protesting and walking out of the schools, the churches were facing the need to speak out about the civil rights of Hispanics. One of the key complaints against schools was prohibition of use of Spanish on the school grounds. As an institution itself sustained by a commitment to Spanish-language ministry, the Conference should clearly support such grievances, but would it?

This was the period when Mexican American farmworkers intensified their drive to organize labor unions. With an enormous farmworker population in Texas, this issue would surface dramatically. How would the local churches and Annual Conference respond?

For too many churches and individuals, these questions were appropriate matters for politicians and government, not for the church. The church's mission was to be confined to saving souls, not to affirming people's rights through declarations or action. Another prevailing response was that other church institutions should address these issues: "That's what community centers and community programs are for." The local church, many insisted, was not "equipped" for dealing with these questions and needs.

But there were a few others. Their response was that all these concerns were a call to ministry for every church and every Christian. They affirmed that, ready or not, these calls from the poor, the students, the farmworkers, were God's own calling to the Conference and the churches. The writer of this chapter feels deeply that this latter response was a sign to many young laity and clergy to stay within the institution rather than leave it.

In summary, the period from merger in 1939 to the creation of The United Methodist Church in 1968 was an exciting one for the Río Grande Conference. Numerical growth, strengthened programming, and increased financial giving were hallmarks of the time. With patience and compassion, the merged Conference sought to include and affirm all the groups that became a part of it. And as the period drew to a close, the social and cultural context pressed new questions of mission that demanded response.

SELF-DETERMINATION AND THE END OF ISOLATION (1968 to the Present)

It is against the backdrop of a cultural renaissance known as the Chicano movement that one can appreciate the events in the Río Grande Conference during the 1964–68 quadrennium. The movement's early slogan, "Ya basta!" (enough), characterized the increasing impatience that Hispanics, especially the young, were feeling with society's institutions, including the church. Throughout the Southwest, in the schools, the fields, the universities, and the churches, the Chicano movement challenged established institutions to respect the history, culture, and values of Hispanic people. They sought to have their gifts and contributions acknowledged and welcomed into the common life of the region and the country.

The two developments that reached their climax in 1964–67 were the question of the Conference relationship to general agency decision making and the equally urgent question of the future structure for ministry to Mexican Americans. These developments responded to two crucial issues that the Conference had never resolved for itself. One issue, the administration of the resources made available by the National Division, had been an increasing source of tension and frustration for nearly two decades. This problem was aggravated by the broad charter given to the Office of Spanish-Speaking Work, based in San Antonio in 1948. The resolution of this challenge has been noted above.

The other issue faced and resolved by the Conference was the question of its continuance as an Annual Conference and its relationship to the other geographic Conferences.

A 1957 research study by the National Division entitled "Methodism in the Río Grande Conference" had concluded that merger was "inevitable." Indeed, the Latin American Provisional Conference in California and Arizona had been merged into the geographic Conferences in 1956. Coincidentally, the Presbyterian Mexican American unit in Texas was absorbed into the English-speaking presbyteries in Texas in 1955. All of these events gave impetus to the expectations that merger of the Río Grande Conference into the other Conferences in the region was somehow inevitable. In the midst of these events, and running counter to the prevailing wisdom, the Río Grande Conference resisted all invitations to consider merger throughout the 1950s.

With the steady progress in elimination of the Central Jurisdiction during the early 1960s, new questions were raised about the continued existence of the Río Grande Conference. By the mid-1960s some of the results of the previous mergers in California were becoming evident.

It was in this period that the Conference decided to study *for itself* its options for the future, including the possibility of merger. This study was to gauge the attitudes, ideas, thinking, and preferences of the Río Grande laity and clergy primarily. The thinking and opinions of persons outside the Conference were sought and received. A study committee was elected in 1964 to undertake this task during the 1964–68 quadrennium under the leadership of the Reverend Roy D. Barton.

The final report was rendered at the 1967 session of the Annual Conference and adopted unanimously. Its central feature was the recommendation that the Río Grande Conference should continue as an Annual Conference. The actual wording was "It is the consensus of the Study Committee that we should continue as an Annual Conference. This does not preclude the possibility of a different structure in the future which may be better suited and needed for more effective ministry."

A related recommendation called for increased cooperation with the neighboring Annual Conferences in serving the needs of Spanish-speaking people in Texas and New Mexico.

The resolution of these two issues brought a new sense of self-respect and mutuality in the Río Grande Conference's relationship with the denomination. There was a sense that justified complaints had been listened to—that the Conference had determined *for itself* its best future within the denomination. For the first time in their history, Mexican American Methodists had significant decision-making authority within a structure they had chosen.

The 1970s was a period of expanding horizons and widening contacts with the larger Hispanic church community and indeed the whole denomination. At the very dawn of the decade, the Hispanic United Methodist Church leadership organized into a national caucus, MARCHA (Methodists Associated Representing the Cause of Hispanic Americans). This group grew out of concerns and frustrations with the level of responsiveness of the church to Hispanic ministries and issues. The original steering committee of MARCHA was organized in San Antonio in December 1970. Four persons from the Río Grande Conference were placed on this initial steering committee. The initial phase of

MARCHA was to culminate in the first national gathering of Hispanic Methodists in the history of the United States, in May of 1971 at El Paso, Texas. The Río Grande Conference served as host to this national meeting and was fully involved in its planning.

The Conference also participated in two events during 1970–71 that were to give it direction in its future relations with the church at large. Through its Conference Board of Global Ministries, the Annual Conference developed in the spring of 1970 a series of major program proposals to be presented to the National Division of the General Board of Missions. This was the first opportunity for Conference representatives to make their case directly to a general agency in the Methodist connection. A similar opportunity was offered in September of 1971 during the General Board of Missions meeting in Los Angeles. On this occasion, Conference representatives, along with MARCHA leadership, called on the General Board to respond with policies, programs, and funding adequate to the needs of Hispanic people in communities and churches.

During the decade of the 1970s, the Conference developed more effective and more participatory planning for ministry. The establishment of program councils, later the Council on Ministries, at the Conference and district levels permitted more persons to have "ownership" of programming. The long distances and infrequent contacts between areas of the Conference made this new sense of participation very important in enlisting support for Conference plans and budgets. A significant goal-setting and planning effort occurred in 1973–75. This process included hearings throughout the Conference area. Hundreds of persons participated. The steering committee of the study, under the staff leadership of the Reverend Dan Rodríguez, the Council Director, developed ten-year Conference goals. Two of the most significant were the recruitment of ordained ministers and the achievement of financial self-support. The resulting document, "New opportunities for the Future," became a manual for guiding Conference priorities. Almost concurrently, in 1973–76 the Conference engaged in a three-year Stewardship Crusade. The financial goal of $150,000 for salaries and pensions was surpassed. The

Reverend Raúl Quintanilla provided able staff leadership in this effort.

As these Conference programming and financial goals were being met, the context of mission and ministry was changing. New claims by newly awakened constituencies were emerging. These constituencies included the urban poor, the undocumented, farmworkers, the more activist students, and women. All of them called on the church to respond to their cause in one way or another. The Annual Conference engaged in spirited and sometimes rancorous debate on the appropriate response to the claims of these groups. Its laity and clergy responded in a variety of ways. Early on, for instance, the Conference endorsed the grape and lettuce boycotts called by the United Farmworkers. In the lower Río Grande Valley the district superintendents, Alfred T. Grout and José Galindo, took decisive stands in support of the efforts of farmworkers to organize. They were not supported by all clergy and laity, however. In San Antonio the first successful community organization among Hispanics, COPS, began with a sizable grant from United Methodists. The Reverend Daniel Rodríguez was a member of the original steering committee. Likewise, urban mission efforts in Houston and El Paso were led by United Methodist ministers: in Houston, by Arturo Fernández; in El Paso, by Conrado Soltero. A similar effort in Dallas, with Rubén Salcido as director, was funded by the General Commission on Religion and Race. However, only minimal Conference financial support was ever given to these projects.

During the 1970s, the General Commission on the Status and Role of Women (COSROW) was organized. Conference leadership for COSROW was provided by Lydia Sáenz, at the time a laywoman from Houston. For the first time, there was monitoring of the participation of women in Conference and district agencies. In the midst of resistance, the women persistently challenged the Conference for full participation. One result of these efforts was the election of the first Hispanic woman to General Conference in 1980, Mrs. Noemí Janes. Previously, in 1964, Mrs. May Alvírez, a former missionary and pastor's wife, had been elected.

At the beginning of the 1980's, the Conference would be a key participant and resource in the Consulta Fronteriza, sponsored by the National Division of the General Board of Global Ministries. This consultation would become the principal arena in which the Annual Conference would respond to the issues of the border. Key leadership was given by Hispanics, including Dr. David Maldonado and the Reverend Joel Martínez.

As the 1980s closed, one could point to areas in the ministry of the Río Grande Conference that give cause for hope. The following are only indicative of these, not exhaustive:

- The impetus to recruitment of clergy and diaconal ministers by the Conference Office of Recruitment. The office was created at the enthusiastic urging of Dr. Josué González, who was its first director.
- The excellent lay administrators program, jointly sponsored by the Annual Conference and the Mexican American Program at Perkins School of Theology. Led by Dr. Roy D. Barton, this program has nurtured lay leadership, which has strengthened the Conference at all levels.
- The Congregational Development Program, established in 1986. This effort continues the congregational planning study of 1982–85. This program, staffed by the Reverend José Palos, promises much for church development and revitalization.
- The Conference Pension Crusade of 1984–88. The $600,000 goal was oversubscribed by over $100,000 in a time of economic difficulty throughout the Southwest. The willingness of people to give to a cause that is clearly related to the sacrificial service of those who served so admirably is a further sign of the vitality and generosity of a people who have not forgotten.
- The appointment of the first woman to serve as district superintendent in the Conference, the Reverend Minerva Carcaño. This was a clear indication that the Conference was moving forward with vision and openness to God's calling.
- The efforts to elect a Conference member to the episcopacy are continuing. Since 1972, when Roy D. Barton and Roberto Escamilla received the first significant votes, the Annual

Conference has pursued this goal. It is not yet achieved; however, the harboring and nurturing of the expectation is a sign of hope.

The more recent period in the Río Grande Conference history has been unprecedented in the demands faced by the Conference as an institution. It has had to respond to jurisdictional and general church levels of involvement in new ways. It has had to collaborate with the national Hispanic United Methodist constituency in a closer relationship. It has had to develop a more comprehensive approach in its planning and programming. And it has faced multiplying demands from various constituencies for its resources and support. Generally, the Conference has sought to be responsive even at the risk of internal struggle and dissent.

The Río Grande Conference will endure as a viable institution to the degree that it responds to Hispanic people's deepest needs and aspirations. The Conference must not see itself as "just another Annual Conference." It is more than a United Methodist organizational unit. It is a Hispanic people's institution. In meeting its United Methodist obligations, it dare not ignore its people's pain and promise!

3

THE WESTERN JURISDICTION

Félix Gutiérrez

The story of the Methodist Church in the Spanish-speaking communities of Arizona and California is filled with good intentions and mutual suspicions, efforts that succeeded and failed, and hopes for a better life through Christ on both sides. It has not always been an easy relationship, but it is one that has endured for more than a century as the region moved from its status as newly conquered Mexican territory to providing key states in the Sunbelt.

1826–1910: SOWING THE SEEDS OF METHODISM

The seeds of organized Methodism were not sown in Arizona and California until after the United States militarily occupied the territories in the 1846 war against Mexico. At that time, the aggressive and enthusiastic Methodists organized English-speaking congregations up and down California and also established missions for Native Americans and Chinese. But they apparently did not begin organized outreach to the area's many Spanish-speaking residents.

Early Hispanic Work in Arizona

Although records are incomplete, it is clear that Latino Methodism reached into Arizona by the 1870s, when the

Methodist Episcopal Church's New Mexico Annual Conference had under its jurisdiction the Southwest Spanish Mission, covering Arizona east of meridian 112, New Mexico, Colorado, El Paso, and the Mexican states of Chihuahua and Sonora. According to José Moreno Fernández, whose 1973 doctoral dissertation is the key research document on the history of Hispanic Methodism in southern California and Arizona, the missionary effort brought Methodist ministers from New Mexico into remote mission outposts in eastern Arizona.

Before the 1890s the Methodist Episcopal Church, South, was working among Arizona Latinos. Its Northwest Mexico Mission Conference, covering the Mexican states of Chihuahua, Sonora, and Durango, had a congregation in Phoenix by 1890. The records of that Conference's 1893 meeting in El Paso list the Reverend Emeterio Quiñones as minister of the Phoenix church. In 1896 the Reverend S. U. Dilly was pastor in Nogales, and in 1897 the Reverend H. C. Hernández was appointed to the Tucson church. In 1903 the Reverend Lawrence Reynolds, who had served as a missionary in Mexico, began visiting Tempe and holding Methodist services in private homes.

In a speech given at the seventieth anniversary of Primera Iglesia Metodista de Phoenix, the Reverend Esaú P. Muñoz, who served churches in Mexico, Texas, Arizona, and California from 1914 to 1948, recounted the early efforts of the city's Mexican residents to learn about Methodism before 1890:

They often preached in the open air, where the curious came to see what Protestants believed. This was in 1890. . . . A family surnamed Orozco, that lived apart from the town, . . . often came to listen to the Protestants. . . . The missionaries, seeing their constancy, linked them with a visitor whose name was Elliott, and who turned out to be a Methodist worker from somewhere in South America who spoke Spanish.

Joseph Irvine, a member of the *congregación americana,* gave a plot of land in the southern part of the city for the building of a Mexican chapel under the direction of Elliott, Muñoz recounted. But the actual construction of the chapel was conducted by the Mexicans. The new chapel gave the Spanish-speaking Methodists a place to meet, but they had not waited for its construction to begin holding their own services, which had been taken place in the Orozco's yard.

In rural eastern Arizona Protestant services were held in Sánchez, in the Gila River Valley area, prior to 1900, but no formal organized efforts were made until around 1905, when the Southwest Spanish Mission of the New Mexico Annual Conference sent two ministers, the Reverend Leandro Fernández and the Reverend Dionicio Costales, into the region. They built an adobe chapel on the banks of the Gila River and held regular Sunday services attended by as many as fifty people, until the chapel was destroyed by a flood around 1918.

The need for work among Mexicans in Arizona was apparently not lost on the local leadership of the northern Methodist Episcopal Church. But despite recognition of the need and opportunity, apparently most of the efforts, save for establishing a school for "Spanish girls" in Tucson in 1908, went toward organizing English-speaking congregations.

Early Work in Southern California

Apparently the first concerted efforts to win southern California Latinos to Methodism followed a 1879 resolution at the Methodist Episcopal Church's Southern California Conference calling for the investigation of the possibility of establishing a Spanish mission. The following year, in September 1880, as Methodist Episcopal leaders met at the Annual Conference in Los Angeles, Antonio Díaz, Spanish missionary in Los Angeles, addressed the Conference in Spanish and was translated by W. F. Wenk. According to the Conference record, in its last business item of the meeting the Conference heard from the head of a committee on the Spanish Mission. Reporting on the first year of progress, the committee noted that the work had been under the direction of the Committee on Missions of the Fort St. Methodist Episcopal Church, had been connected with the Florence Mission since April, and had received a $500 donation from the Missionary Board. The mission was renting a small chapel on

Rose Street for $8 a month, was paying Antonio Díaz $160 for his services, and had formed a committee to "secure a permanent location of a Mission Church."

The following year, when Methodist leaders met in Santa Barbara the Conference appointments included "Spanish Work" missions in Los Angeles and Santa Barbara, but the names of the pastors of these missions were listed as "To Be Supplied." Although Díaz is not mentioned by name, the annual report of the Los Angeles superintendent reported continued progress.

In his report, Santa Barbara District Presiding Elder W. A. Knighten praised the abilities and work of brother Juan Martínez, who organized the Spanish Mission in that district with six men, seven women, and fourteen children at the Santa Barbara church.

In his final report for 1881, C. G. Belknap, head of the Committee on Missions, asked the presiding bishop to secure additional funds for Spanish-speaking work, this time suggesting "there ought to be a special appropriation of at least $5,000 to establish and man a Spanish Mission within the bounds of this Conference. This work within our territory is of such importance that we ought to take advanced ground at once." Recommending a bold course of action that would not be acted upon for another thirty years, the committee also urged the appointment of a superintendent of Spanish Mission work and warned "to neglect this field longer is rendering us liable of incurring the Divine displeasure."

But the plea for sufficient funds was not answered by the church leaders who could have provided the needed financial support. The work continued in Santa Barbara, where Presiding Elder W. A. Knighten reported that missionary Juan B. Martínez continued preaching in the streets, visiting from house-to-house and raising the ire of Roman Catholic priests, "who became aroused and opposed the work with persistent and malignant fury." Without sufficient support from Methodist Episcopal missionary agencies, the work among southern California's Mexicans was apparently allowed to lapse after 1882.

Because records of early Methodist efforts among Mexicans are scattered and incomplete, it is impossible to identify or recount the story of each pioneer preacher and congregation. Perhaps the story of Santiago H. Limbs, a Mexican from Texas whose story was told in a 1949 edition of *El Mensajero Metodista*, will help convey the struggles and successes of many of the early Methodist ministers. He was a Methodist preacher from Texas whose preaching awakened the interest of some English-speaking churches. They organized an Interdenominational Society for his support, which was set at four or five dollars a week.

Within a short time the work had spread eastward into the rural communities of Pomona, Redlands, San Bernandino, and other places near Los Angeles. Limbs continued this work until 1898, when he organized the Spanish American Society to spread the work to other counties around Los Angeles. The following year he moved to El Rio in Ventura County north of Los Angeles, where he established congregations throughout the county. Leaving the El Rio church under the pastorship of Domingo Mata, he returned to Los Angeles in 1899. There he organized another church, which he pastored until 1904. After A. G. Lerma assumed the pastorate of the Los Angeles church in that year, Limbs returned to Ventura County. The 1902 Annual Conference reported on Limbs's progress but also noted that more church support was needed to finance the mission effort.

In addition to Los Angeles and Ventura counties, successful missions were established in Redlands, Pasadena, Santa Ana, and San Diego between 1900 and 1910. In 1903 the Redlands Mission, which also served Riverside, San Bernandino, Colton, and Ontario, was reported as being headed by a former South American missionary, the Reverend Paul Penzotti. Membership was reported at seventy-six, with Sabbath attendance averaging forty-five and eighty-five dollars in contributions from mission members during the year. But by 1910, when A. G. Lerma headed the effort, the district superintendent reported the work was handicapped because "the Mexicans are nomadic to a great extent, here today and gone tomorrow."

The need for Mexicans to travel to find work in agriculture was also a problem in Pasadena, where the Reverend O. C. Laizure and, later, the Reverend R. A. Weaver developed one of the strongest Spanish-speaking congregations. A small mission church had been built, and a corner lot had been purchased by 1909 for the construction of a new church.

Early Work in Northern California

Records of early work in northern California are less complete than those for Southern California but indicate an interest on the part of some Methodist Episcopal leaders in working with the Spanish-speaking people. As early as the 1850s Methodists had supported missionary efforts among Germans. By 1890 the Conference also had efforts to reach Japanese, Norwegians, Danes, Swedes, and Hawaiians in northern California, but made no mention of Mexicans in its annual report. This omission was not accepted by all church leaders, some of whom had urged outreach to Spanish-speaking Californians. Yet twenty years later, in 1910, the California Annual Conference still had no mention of Spanish work among its appointments or missions but had added Portuguese, Finns, and Italians to the groups previously mentioned.

Characteristics of Early Work in Arizona and California

However well intentioned, the church's efforts to reach Spanish-speaking people were scattered and uncoordinated. Unlike the efforts to reach Chinese, Indians, blacks, and members of various language minority groups, neither regional nor national agencies had a comprehensive plan of outreach to the Mexicans left behind after Arizona and California were taken from Mexico, or those who would cross the border in later years. In analyzing the early period it is possible to identify three types of support for Methodism's outreach to Latinos in Arizona and California.

Interestingly enough, one source of missionary support was Mexico, where the Methodist Episcopal Church, South, had begun missionary work in 1872, and the Methodist Episcopal Church the following year. Some of the missionaries and ministers of both Methodist branches who served Latino churches in California and Arizona, both Anglo and Mexican, had begun their work in Mexico before their assignments to develop Hispanic Methodism in the United States.

Another source of institutional support was (or could have been) missionary efforts, both regional and national. In the last half of the nineteenth century both California and Arizona were seen as unsettled, fertile territories recently conquered from Mexico. But efforts to reach Mexicans were not consistent.

A third source of support was Anglo Methodist congregations. In Los Angeles, Santa Barbara, Phoenix, and elsewhere, local Methodist leaders and congregations assisted in the organizing of Mexican churches through their financial contributions, sharing of facilities, and personal support.

1911–19: THE FORMATIVE PERIOD OF REGIONAL EFFORTS

By 1910 Methodist efforts to reach Mexicans in Arizona and California had found considerable success where they had been adequately funded and staffed. But another, more potent force was also to influence the growth of the Spanish-speaking Methodist Church. This was the Mexican Revolution of 1910, which would be the impetus for immigration into the southwestern United States at a time when growers, mining companies, and factories were looking for cheap, hardworking labor. Along with the search for a better life, some of these immigrants would bring a background of interest in Protestantism; in some cases, some were Protestant ministers trained in Mexico. This injection of Mexican growth and leadership, coupled with the Methodist congregations and ministers already in service, set the foundation for expansion and growth.

Southern California

The person selected to direct the Spanish-speaking effort in this period of growth for southern California was Vernon McCombs,

71

a former missionary in Peru who returned to Los Angeles in 1911 because of ill health and was named Superintendent of Spanish Work for the Southern California Annual Conference in 1911. Working from an office in South Pasadena, in 1912 McCombs added efforts in Anaheim and Santa Ana to the existing churches in Los Angeles and Pasadena.

The data in table 3.1, compiled by the author and by José Fernández (1973 dissertation) from Southern California Conference Annual Reports, chart much of the growth in the period in which McCombs headed what became the Conference's Spanish and Portuguese District in 1913.

Table 3.1. Expansion of Hispanic Work, 1912–19

Year	Members	New Locations of Work
1912	98 members	Santa Ana, Anaheim, Rivera, Montebello, Downey, Compton, Los Angeles, Pasadena
1913	220 members	Lankershim, Santa Paula, Fullerton
1914	Unreported	Santa Monica, Watts, El Modena, Long Beach
1915	241 members	Placentia, Fillmore, Ventura, Olinda, Hanford, Tulare, Ingomar, Artesia, Westminster, San Pedro
1916	285 members	San Fernando, Los Angeles Plaza, Yorba, Huntington Beach
1917	345 members	Watts, Puente, Calexico Circuit, Zaferia, Lamanda Park, Glendale, San Fernando Valley
1918	724 members	Orange, Garden Grove, La Habra, Saticoy, Bardsdale
1919	644 members	Talbert, Newport, Wilmington, Moorpark, Glendora, El Monte, Etiwanda, Upland, Cucamonga

In 1918 the district superintendents reported that forty-three persons were trained or being trained for Spanish work and that the Latin American work in California was almost equally staffed by Anglos and Latinos, with twenty salaried Mexicans and twenty-one Americans. Among the ministers working in the Spanish and Portuguese District in 1917 and 1918 were Enrique Narro, Luis P. Tirre, J. C. Nava, Ricardo Shade, Emilio Hernández, José L. Tavares, Alfonso Sánchez, E. M. Sein, A. C. Gonzales, Vicente Mendoza, L. C. Flores, and Antonio Jiménez.

Not directly related to the development of the Hispanic churches but important in Methodism's outreach to the growing Mexican population in southern California was the growth and development of four Methodist-related institutions between 1900 and 1920. These were the Spanish American Institute, an industrial training school for Mexican boys; the Frances DePauw Home, a boarding school for Mexican girls; Goodwill Industries, a sheltered workshop for people of all races; and the Plaza Community Center, a social welfare agency in East Los Angeles.

Since southern California Methodists defined their Hispanic outreach as a missionary effort, it is not unusual that an Anglo with a missionary background was chosen to head the effort. However, in offering the leadership opportunity to McCombs, the Methodists overlooked indigenous Hispanic Methodist leaders who were also well suited to lead the work among their own people.

Fernández points out in his dissertation that unlike the indigenous leadership, McCombs looked upon his Mexican charges as an outsider would and sometimes took on a paternalistic attitude. "Let us look at their pale, pinched faces with Christ-like compassion," he said; he asked Anglo Methodists to remember that "from us they got their birth. . . . They must look to us for eternal life." Although his writings demonstrated more compassion than did those of Anglos who merely looked upon Mexicans as a "problem people," McCombs also supported Americanization as an avenue that the church should promote among the Mexicans.

The Methodist Episcopal Church, South, in Arizona and California

More realistic was the approach of the Methodist Episcopal Church, South, which did not allow the border between the United States and Mexico to divide its ministry among Mexicans in both countries. Using an integrated approach, the General Conference meeting in Oklahoma City in 1914 formed the Pacific Mexican Mission, with responsibilities for the Mexican states of Sonora, Sinaloa, Tepic, the Mexican territory of Baja California, and Mexican work in Arizona and California. While much of the work took place in Texas, the Methodist Episcopal Church, South, also had active efforts in Arizona and California. This binational approach would continue until the reunion of 1939.

At its fifth annual session in El Paso in 1918, the Pacific Mexican Mission reported Western District pastors serving in Phoenix, Tempe, Ray, Jerome, and Nogales in Arizona. California work included Los Angeles and the Homer Toberman Mission near Los Angeles. It was also reported that work was planned for the Arizona communities of Ajo, Miami, Ray, Hayden, and Superior. In a 1972 interview (cited in Fernández, 1973), Mrs. Carolina Carrasco Oquita recalled that in Douglas religious services led by lay leaders Joaquín Carrasco and Jesús Murrial were held in the home of Mrs. Otilia Valencia. When ministers of the mission later came into the area, they found that Mexican Methodists were already meeting. On this foundation, the Reverend Dionicio Costales was able to build a congregation and church in 1917.

1920–40: THE MISSIONARY ERA

The work among Spanish-speaking groups in the United States had long been seen as a missionary effort. But despite the resolutions and pleadings of local and regional Methodist leaders since at least 1880, the national leadership of the northern Methodist Episcopal Church had not given the work the same recognition given to foreign missions or home missions work among Indians, Asians, and blacks. Finally, in 1920, the General Conference established a regional mission effort, but also combined it with work among non-Hispanic groups.

The Latin American Mission

The mission was launched with McCombs as its superintendent and Vicente Mendoza as Latin American missionary of the Board of Sunday Schools. Initial work was centered in southern California, where several congregations had been developed earlier. At its organizational meeting the Latin American Mission consisted of twenty-five appointments, some of them of circuit ministers serving several communities. Of the twenty-five, twenty-one were designated as Mexican or Latin American, two were Portuguese, one was Italian, and one was bilingual. Twenty-two were in the Southern California Conference, including Bakersfield and Hanford, and three were in the Northern California Conference cities of Oakland, Sacramento, and San Francisco.

The 1920s were years of growth and expansion for the churches and members of the Latin American Mission. Conference reports were filled with detailed descriptions of new members, enthusiastic work, and churches being planned or built. Among them was the Plaza Mexican Church on Los Angeles' La Placita, long the center of the area's Mexican community.

Church Growth

In a 1924 report McCombs noted that while it took eight years to reach 640 members, "During the past five years the number has increased to 1,408 members." He reported that in four years the number of members in Sunday school had increased threefold, total giving fourfold, and persons reached annually tenfold. In 1924 the number of circuit pastorates had doubled to 31, with 79 preaching places, workers increased from 48 to 61, and total church membership increased from 713 to 2,079. Latino Methodists were also generous in their support of the church, with giving increasing from $2,021 to $12,299. With missionary zeal, the Latino Methodists aggressively spread the word and brought others to the church.

Work in Arizona and Northern California

In the mid-1920s the Methodist Episcopal Church also moved its Latin American Mission work eastward into Arizona, long a center of activity for the Methodist Episcopal Church, South. However, leaders of the two Methodist churches continued to fight over who should work among the Mexicans in Arizona.

Growth in the 1930s

Building and expanding on the foundation laid in the 1920s, Hispanic Methodism continued to grow through the 1930s. As in the past, the Methodist effort went beyond traditional church activities and into social, educational, and medical services. It also witnessed increased activity among members of the Federation of Ladies Aid Societies of the Latin American Mission. These societies were also responsible for missionary work among Indians in Mexico.

Another effort was church music, to which notable hymnnologists Dr. Vicente Mendoza and the Reverend Epigmenio Velasco were contributing by writing and translating hymns and anthems during the 1930s. One of the best-known hymns, "Jesús es mi Rey Soberano," continues to be sung in Hispanic churches around the world.

Work of Methodist Episcopal Church, South

As noted earlier, the Methodist Episcopal Church, South, also supported missionary efforts in the region, and these also continued to grow. The Western Mexican Conference supported efforts from El Paso to Los Angeles, including churches in Los Angeles, Inglewood, Clovis, Dinuba, Phoenix, Tempe, Sonora, Miami, Prescott, Tucson, and Nogales in the mid-1930s. The 1935 Conference, held in El Paso, received reports on the activities of 792 members spread across eighteen congregations in Arizona and California.

Many of the activities were the same as those of the northern Methodist Episcopal Church, with Conference committees on Christian education, church construction, temperance, Christian literature, lay activities, hospitals, missions, and evangelism. But the records of the southern church reflected some philosophical differences between the two branches of Methodism. For one thing, unlike the Conference reports of McCombs and his colleagues, the records of the Western Mexican Conference were published and its business was conducted entirely in Spanish.

Impact of Church Unification

In 1939 the Methodist Episcopal Church, the Methodist Episcopal Church, South, and the Methodist Protestant Church united to form the Methodist Church. The unification of the church was accompanied by a reorganization of the Latin American Mission to include both the work of the Latin American Mission of the Methodist Episcopal Church and the Western Mexican Conference of the Methodist Episcopal Church, South.

The new mission was put under McCombs, who reported in 1939 that the effort had 46 workers reaching 4,337 members at 66 preaching points. The Latin American Mission also enrolled 4,036 Sunday school pupils, 1,311 Epworth League members, and 537 members of the Women's Societies. As Fernández notes in his dissertation, the transition also marked the end of the missionary era in Latino Methodism. It came at the same time that the Latino ministers and lay people were demanding a greater voice in running Conference, district, and congregational affairs. These and other forces would set the stage for what Fernández calls the Golden Era of Hispanic Methodism.

1940–54: THE GOLDEN ERA OF HISPANIC METHODISM

Latino ministers set the stage for the Golden Era by putting forth a series of demands, not all of them written down, calling for greater Latino self-determination in the church. These demands, as reported by Fernández, included the following:

1. Appointment of Hispanic ministers for all supervisory positions.
2. Appointment of Hispanics to key boards, committees, or departments.
3. Use of Spanish in conducting all Conference business sessions.
4. Determination of the total program of Hispanic churches by Hispanics themselves.

These and other concerns were partially addressed on July 3, 1941, when Bishop James Chamberlain Baker called on the Reverend S. D. Athens to read a resolution regarding the reorganization of the Latin American Mission into a Provisional Annual Conference, as had been provided for at the 1940 General Conference of the Methodist Church.

The Provisional Conference included eleven appointments and twenty preaching charges in Arizona, twenty-two appointments and forty-three preaching points in southern California, and six appointments to twelve preaching points in northern California. The far-flung territory reached from Douglas in Southern Arizona to Sacramento in northern California. Also included in the work of the provisional Conference were the Spanish American Institute, Plaza Community Center, Homer Toberman Settlement House and Clinic, Latin American Mission, and Frances DePauw Girl's School, all located in Los Angeles or nearby.

McCombs remained as general superintendent until his retirement in 1946, a post he had held with various titles since 1911. There was also an Anglo assistant general superintendent under him, a structure that rankled some Latinos. Also, the request to use Spanish to conduct Conference sessions was denied. In 1946 Luis P. Tirre was named to the top post. For the first time Hispanics were appointed as district superintendents, and some were elected delegates to Jurisdictional Conferences.

The members of the Provisional Conference also saw to it that Spanish was well integrated into the preaching, lessons, and music of the church. Spanish was spoken throughout the church and its activities, except for the business sessions of the Conference. Because of the language, culture, and activities of the church, the Latino Methodist churches played a central role in the lives of their members, in contrast to most Anglo churches.

As in the past, the Latino Methodist Church offered an alternative religious belief structure to members of a predominantly Roman Catholic, Spanish-speaking community. Methodists did not smoke, drink, or do other worldly things such as dance or go to movies. Methodists were also encouraged to enter into a personal relationship to God through Christ. Because of the belief in a better life after death through salvation, Latino Methodists were encouraged to prepare in their life on earth for their life beyond. It was this belief in a better life that helped carry Latino Methodists through difficult personal and social problems. In this period, as in the past, Roman Catholics sometimes took a harsh view of those who joined other churches, often criticizing or ostracizing them.

The active lives of the Latino Methodist churches and their contributions to their communities were reflected on the pages of *La Cadena de Oro* and its successor, *El Mensajero Metodista,* the official organ of the Latin American Provisional Conference during the 1940s and early 1950s. The newspaper reflects a full and rich church, one that is proud of the activities of its local congregations, the contributions of its youths and women, and its efforts to forge links between members in different regions. It is also apparent that youth work was of particular importance, both at the local church level and beyond.

In the Provisional Conference years, between 1941 and 1955, the number of churches stayed at around 40 and members at more than 3,000, with a slow but steady gain to 3,230 by 1955. However, in 1953 the predominantly Anglo Southern California–Arizona Annual Conference had received a report from the Reverend Keith Kanaga and the Reverend Larry Domínguez on the integration of the Latin American Provisional Conference into a nonminority Conference. Among other items, the committee investigating integration promised that uniting the Latino effort with a predominantly Anglo Conference would enhance "Christian brotherhood," increase financial support for the Latin American ministry, encourage young Latinos to enter the ministry, lift the general standards of the Latin American people, facilitate cooperation between Latino and other churches, and provide better supervision for the Latino churches. No negative effects of the proposed integration were mentioned in the report, which recommended that a phased integration be completed by 1957.

But the negative impact of the proposed merger was quickly felt by the Latino churches. In 1955 theHÿüUMPHGD4 encourage young Latinos to enter the ministry, lift the general standards of the Latin American people, facilitate cooperation between Latino and other churches, and provide better supervision for the Latino churches. No negative effects of the proposed integration were mentioned in the report, which recommended that a phased integration be completed by 1957.

But the negative impact of the proposed merger was quickly felt by the Latino churches. In 1955 thefornia–Arizona Annual Conference. But it was a move that ran counter to the Latinos' desire for autonomy and self-determination.

After negotiating such matters as pastors' salary allowances, title to church properties, and payment of pastors' pensions, the Latin American Provisional Conference was terminated on June 18, 1956, and absorbed into predominantly Anglo Conferences. Most members went into the Southern California–Arizona Conference, but those in northern California were transferred to the California-Nevada Conference. These included churches in Bakersfield, Corcoran, Dinuba, Fresno, Mountain View, San José, Sacramento, Stockton, and Selma. Churches in Arizona included Douglas, Nogales, Phoenix, Flagstaff, Prescott, Sonora-Hayden, Tempe-Mesa, and Tucson. Southern California churches were located in Fillmore-Ventura, Long Beach, Santa Monica,

Santa Paula, Watts, Los Angeles, Pasadena, San Fernando, Anaheim, El Modeno, Rivera-Pico, Santa Ana, and Stanton-Artesia.

Whatever the economic realities that made it necessary or the promises that made it attractive, the reality of integration meant that Latinos and their churches became a subpopulation within a larger church agenda.

In 1957, following integration, the Southern California–Arizona Annual Conference heard recommendations on strengthening and extending work among Latinos, allocating funds to churches for Latino work, assigning Latino pastors as associates to Anglo churches, airing "The Methodist Hour" radio program in Spanish, and recruiting ministers for such work. However, such attention was less than it had been under the Mission and the Provisional Conference, when the annual progress of each congregation was reported in detail each year.

In 1958 a Commission on Latin American Work was constituted by the Conference, and the following year its head, Kenneth D. Doctor, warned that integration should not mean that Latinos would be forced to lose their cultural identity or indigenous leadership.

However sincere the effort, integration was a new experience for both Hispanics and Anglos in and out of the Methodist Church. In his dissertation Fernández examined the effect of integration on two well-organized groups from the Provisional Conference era, the Women's Society of Christian Service (WSCS), and the Methodist Youth Fellowship (MYF). He found that initially the twenty-two WSCS Hispanic groups were added to the Conference WSCS roster, the groups exchanged visits, and four elected leaders of the Hispanic WSCS were on the Conference program committee. But later Conference WSCS leaders visited the Hispanic group and told them there could be no separate Hispanic organization. From that date the enthusiasm for continued integration dwindled.

In the case of the MYF, Fernández found that integration meant that Latino youths did not attend camps and other Conference activities in numbers as large as when they were under

Latin Councils. While youth rallies continued in Arizona, youths from that state participated less in camping. Integrating Anglos into the Latin camp was tried for two summers but not continued. Summing up, Fernández wrote: "Integration took place on the conference level on paper, but the Hispanics did not participate in it."

Between 1957 and 1967 the number of Hispanic Methodist churches declined by 10, from 29 to 19; the number of preparatory members in these churches declined by 400, from 989 to 589; and the number of full members declined by 527, from 2,551 to 2,054. Only in total funds paid for all purposes was there an increase, from $84,636 to $152,439. Of the 10 churches that were closed, only 2 were merged into Anglo churches. The other 8 were discontinued.

By the late 1960s it was apparent to both Anglos and Latinos that the integration effort had not been successful at the level that is Methodism's foundation: the local church and its members. Along with the civil rights movement of the period came a renewed militancy on the part of members of all racial minorities and, often, and increased receptiveness to their views on the part of some Anglos with whom they interacted. In 1968 the Southern California–Arizona Conference's Ethnic Strategy Committee issued a lengthy report saying that "integration seen as Angloization is an outmoded concept among Mexican Americans and no longer can be tolerated by our Latin churches."

The report was the first step in a concerted effort to promote Hispanic work among Methodists in the region. Like the demands presented nearly three decades earlier, it came from Hispanic ministers. It came out of (1) the formation of the Latin American Methodist Action Group (LAMAG) at Lake Elsinore in March 1968 and (2) the election of future Bishop Elías Galván as LAMAG's founding president. Although it is too early to assess the impact of this new approach from a historical perspective, it is clear that it had the effect of refocusing work on the local church level, on the needs of local members and pastors, and on the necessity of building Latino leadership from the local church upward into the denominational hierarchy. In 1988, partly as a result of this revitalized interest in Hispanic work, a new structure was created that gave Hispanics a greater sense of identity and mission, and the Reverend Leo D. Nieto was appointed as its superintendent.

In some ways, the 1968 statement helped close the circle that was first drawn in the 1870s when Methodists in Arizona and California launched missionary efforts toward the Spanish-speaking residents. As in the past, the 1968 statement pointed to the great potential for productive work among Latinos. But it also brought closure to the missionary mentality and its successor, integration through assimilation. Rather than accepting an Anglo model, the Hispanic leadership challenged the fundamental thinking of the church and called for others in the region to adapt to the Hispanic reality. It is against this framework that the work that followed should be measured.

Methodist leaders on the West Coast (date unknown). Vernon M. McCombs is first from the left on the second row.

Opening day at the store, Los Angeles Plaza Mexican Church, in 1919.

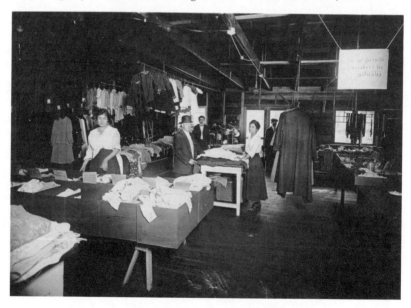

Alejo Hernández
PRIMER MINISTRO METODISTA MEXICANO

Alejo Hernández, the first Methodist Mexican minister.

Pastor and congregation of the Santa Monica Mexican Methodist Church near Los Angeles in the early 1900s.

The original steering committee of MARCHA, 1970.

The United Methodist Church of Knickerbocker was the first church for a Hispanic congregation to be built in the New York Conference.

The Hispanic United Methodist Church of Toledo, Ohio, at worship,1984.

The Reverend Alfredo Cotto-Thorner

>

Dr. Alfredo Nsnez, noted leader and historian of the Rio Grande Conference, visits the tomb of Alejo Henandez on the centennial of his ordination.

The tomb of J. E. A. Vanduzer in Key West, Florida. Died on June 7, 1875. His last words: "Do not abandon the Cuban mission."

The Reverend Juan Sosa

The Reverend Charles W. Drees, founder of Methodist work in Puerto Rico.

Mrs. Antonia M. de Pereles, the first president of the Women's Societies of Puerto Rico.

The Reverend Tomás Rico Soltero, first Puerto Rican superintendent.

4

THE SOUTHEASTERN JURISDICTION

Humberto Carrazana

During the first one hundred years of relations with Methodism, Hispanics in Florida were almost exclusively Cuban in origin, with the first exceptions becoming noticeable in the last twenty-five years. The history of the Florida peninsula and the island of Cuba was the same, from the discovery of America until the last century, when Spain ceded to the United States what is now the state of Florida. The activities of the resident Hispanics, most of them natives of Florida, continued uninterrupted.

But the great avalanche of Cubans began in 1868 with the beginning of the Ten Years' War, launched by Carlos Manuel de Céspedes and other Cuban leaders. The oppression became intolerable, and thousands of Cubans had no option but to go to the battlefields or emigrate. Key West, Tampa, New York, and Philadelphia welcomed them, since there were already Hispanic communities there.

Among the Cubans who had to leave was a rich cigar manufacturer named Francisco Martínez-Ybor, who first decided to open a branch in and then moved his operation to Key West. Most of his workers and their families came with him, thus increasing the population of the Key and giving impetus to the tobacco industry. Later Martínez-Ybor moved his headquarters to Tampa, leaving his name to an important neighborhood that is still known as Ybor City, where he built thousands of homes for his employees.

By 1885 there were in Key West more than eighty Cuban enterprises, both large and small, with more than 10,000 Cuban employees. At that time Key West was one of the main cities of Florida, with churches, masonic lodges, social clubs, schools, and newspapers whose constituencies were exclusively Cuban. The famous club San Carlos was inaugurated in November 1871, and its first president was Luis Someillán, a member of a distinguished Protestant family. Cubans participated actively in politics. Carlos M. de Céspedes, Jr. (the son of the Cuban Father of the Motherland), was elected mayor of Key West in 1876. Monroe County was represented in the legislature by such Cubans as Morúa P. Delgado, Dr. Manuel R. Moreno, and J. G. Pompez. Many came to occupy important positions both in the state and federal governments and in the judiciary system.

The second center of importance in the beginnings of work in Florida was Tampa, where Cuban immigration patterns were similar to those of Key West, especially after Martínez-Ybor moved his factory in 1886. At that time Cubans were specialists in rolling Havana-style cigars by hand. With time, the Cuban community in Tampa, where there was more opportunity for growth, overtook that in Key West. Cubans in Tampa followed the pattern of establishing their own social clubs, lodges, schools, churches, newspapers, and so forth.

Hispanic immigration to Florida during the present century bears the same characteristics; that is, it is mostly composed of Cubans who have come for political reasons. The political reasons mentioned are oppressive dictatorships such as those of Machado and Batista, who ruled over Cuba during most of the period from 1926 to 1940. The hope of returning to the Motherland, even though it may never have materialized, became an obsession for the Cuban population, shaping many of its activities and plans.

It was also during that period that the center of Hispanic population changed from Key West and Tampa to Miami and south Florida, where there were already some 20,000 Puerto Ricans. After 1959, with the repeated waves of emigration from Cuba and Central America (especially from Nicaragua and El Salvador, due to the oppression in those countries), the demographics of this area experienced rapid change. Other Central Americans as well as Colombians, Venezuelans, Chileans, and others have also come, in smaller numbers and for various reasons, thus augmenting the area's Hispanic population. In the counties of Dade and Broward alone there has been an increase from some 50,000 to 1.5 million Hispanics.

Naturally, with this sort of population concentration, Hispanic participation in politics is significant. On July 4, 1986, as part of the festivities connected with the centennial and restoration of the Statue of Liberty, all records were broken in Dade County in the number of new citizens naturalized in a single ceremony: 14,183, mostly Cuban in origin. Sixty-six percent of these registered in the Republican party and were eager to participate in the elections that were then upcoming. The ideological differences between the two major parties do not seem to be the main reasons why Cuban Americans prefer the Republican party. The main cause is the policy of the Republican administration on international matters, especially those having to do with Cuba and Nicaragua.

THE BEGINNINGS: CONGREGATIONS AND SOCIAL CENTERS

The Methodist Church was one of the first Protestant churches to gain converts among the Cuban emigrates in Key West, and very early the need was felt to give them greater attention. In the Florida Annual Conference session of 1873, Dr. Charles A. Fulwood was appointed to Stone Church, with instructions to serve the Cuban population. A young minister who had just been admitted on trial, José E. A. Vanduzer, was appointed as his associate and missionary to the Cuban population. There was also brother Francisco Díaz, who did not have ministerial training but who had awakened the interest and gained the conversion of many people as a biblical colporteur. Less than a year after his appointment, on June 7, 1875, young Vanduzer died a victim of yellow fever. His last words were "Do not abandon the Cuban mission." This challenge remained in the hearts of all.

Among the young people in the congregation there were two Cuban exiles, Enrique and Eduardo Someillán. Enrique would eventually become a well-educated minister and have a very fruitful ministry in Florida and Cuba. Another young convert who would eventually become a minister was Aurelio Silvera. These two continued the work in Stone Church and planned for a school. Since support was insufficient, both also had to work at secular jobs. Silvera returned to his home in Havana, but Enrique Someillán continued the work in Key West. By 1877 the group had acquired its own church on Duval Street, La Trinidad, with the help of Bishop Pierce and a contribution of $1,000 from the Missionary Society. At the Annual Conference of 1887 Someillán was appointed pastor in charge, and in the session of January 1889 there was an extensive report on the progress of the work.

The Reverend Someillán was followed by the Reverend Albert D. Atkin (1894–95) and the Reverend Manuel Deulofeo (1896–1900). (The latter returned to Cuba at the end of Spanish rule and there continued his ministry.) Over the years, the work in Key West grew slowly but firmly.

A Sunday school in a Key West neighborhood gave rise to a new congregation with the purchase of a former Episcopal church on Virginia street. The new church was called El Salvador, and its first pastor was the Reverend Francisco Boán (December of 1917). La Trinidad and El Salvador continued until 1932, when the former was deactivated. During the pastorate of the Reverend César Benítez (1960–66) a church building and a parsonage were built on Virginia Street for El Salvador Church.

The beginnings of Hispanic work in Tampa were similar to those in Key West. Although the Cubans there were mostly Catholics, they were unhappy about the position of their church and clergy, who supported Spanish rule over the island. First Methodist Church in Tampa had begun its missionary work in 1892 among the poorest and neediest of these immigrants, offering them food, clothing, and shelter and teaching them English. The Women's Missionary Society supported a missionary for this work, whose last name was Hammerly. At the Conference of 1894 Someillán was appointed as Tampa

Superintendent of Hispanic work. By 1896 that work already had three Hispanic congregations—one in Ybor City and two in West Tampa—and their three related schools. Ms. M. A. Wolff was superintendent of the schools, and Ms. Rosa Valdés, Ms. Emelina Valdés, and Ms. May Lockard were teachers. These schools developed social service programs for the community, eventually becoming the centers that still preserve the names of these early workers.

Pastoral appointments (Acts of 1913) of the Tampa District, under the heading of "Cuban-Spanish Mission," included the following: West Tampa, San Mateo—the Reverend Guillermo Pérez; Ybor City, San Marcos—the Reverend D. Carrera; East Tampa, San Lucas—J. Figueras, supply; Robert City, San Juan—the Reverend Juan J. Rodríguez, supply; and a missionary to Cuba, the Reverend M. Domínguez. It is also interesting to note that in the Acts of the following year one finds for the first time a Florida Latin District with five churches in Tampa, two in Key West, two Italian congregations, and two missionaries to Cuba, the Reverend Ignacio González and the Reverend N. J. Castellanos. The Reverend J. D. Lewis, who had been a missionary in Cuba, was named presiding elder, as district superintendents were called at that time.

All these various congregations reflected the economic vicissitudes of the tobacco industry and the unavoidable social and political changes of the time, including World War I. With the change of dictatorships from Machado to Batista in Cuba, beginning in August of 1933, a new Cuban exodus began, which settled mostly in Miami. La Trinidad church was closed in 1932–33. At the same time the gravitational center of population passed over to Miami, and a new Hispanic mission was begun there in Trinity Church. Apparently this is historically the first Protestant work among Hispanics in Miami.

When the three main branches of Methodism merged in 1939, the Latin District was dissolved, and the existing congregations were incorporated into the appropriate geographical districts of the Conference. It is difficult to tell whether this change was the result of the early signs of a slowdown in Hispanic work or was rather the cause of that slowdown during the next twenty years.

The Church of the Evangelical United Brethren, which in 1968 would become part of what is now The United Methodist Church, began in 1942 a mission among the Hispanics of Ybor City with the Reverend Plutarco Roa and his wife, who had earlier served as missionaries in Colombia. Their work resulted in the organization of the Iglesia San Pablo in April of 1946 and the founding of the school of the same name. Today that school serves not only Hispanics, but also the community in general.

Toward the end of the decade of the 1940s, three congregations in Tampa merged: San Pablo (Italian in origin), San Lucas, and San Marcos (the latter two Hispanic). In the merger the name of San Marcos was kept. But this effort proved fruitless given the constant ethnic and cultural change in the community. The Annual Conference of 1961 declared this congregation inactive.

The United Methodist Church continued serving the needs of the community, as may be seen in the history of the two social centers there. These centers, jointly with San Pablo school, are under the administration of Tampa United Methodist Centers. When thousands of Cubans from Mariel reached Tampa in April of 1980, the willingness of our church to serve and its efficiency in doing so was shown once again. Presently there are in Tampa two Hispanic congregations: San Pablo and Fe. The latter began as a mission of Tampa Heights United Methodist Church and for some time was connected with Tampa's Nebraska Avenue Church.

Work among Hispanics in Miami began during the Conference year of 1932–33 as a mission of Trinity Methodist Church, whose pastor was the Reverend L. Oser. The Methodists were the first to respond to the needs of a growing Hispanic colony, mostly Puerto Rican in origin. The Reverend Felipe Llera and his wife came over from the Cuba Annual Conference in 1938–39, thus giving impetus to the mission. In a cooperative effort among the Florida Conference, the Miami District, and the National Women's Division of the General Board of Missions, a beautiful church, kindergarten, and child care center, with adjoining buildings including apartments for deaconesses, were built. The facilities included land for recreation and parking. A parsonage was built later. For the inauguration of these facilities in 1948, the Reverend Sergio Alfaro and the congregation he led made their contribution by purchasing furniture and equipment with a great deal of enthusiasm and sacrifice. Under the names of Methodist Hispanic American Church and Latin Methodist Center, during the next twenty years this was the only Hispanic congregation with its own facilities and independent pastoral charge.

As the first massive wave of political exiles arrived between 1959 and 1962, and with the support of the Methodist Committee on Overseas Relief, a Methodist refugee center and a temporary home were organized for young exiles, and these helped thousands of Cubans who arrived penniless. The Reverend and Mrs. C. D. Stewart, the Reverend and Mrs. John Stroud, and missionaries Lorraine Buck, Frances Gaby, Sara Fernández, and Agnes Malloy (the latter in Tampa), who were forced to leave Cuba, worked together with volunteer lay people such as Silvio Pérez, Almiro López, and Olga López, and many more, tending to the needs of the refugees.

After the failed invasion of the Bay of Pigs (April 1961), the Cuban exodus intensified; thousands of Methodist lay people and a number of pastors emigrated. The resulting emergency situation challenged the Methodist church, and particularly some congregations in Miami. Bishop Henley, elected in 1960 and appointed to serve Florida and Cuba, requested the help of all the churches in Florida in establishing an emergency fund that made it possible to employ some of the refugee pastors to serve their own people. The office of the Methodist refugee center was moved to Miami's White Temple Methodist Church (no longer in existence), and the Reverend Stroud, based in Riverside Church of Miami, worked tirelessly to find shelter and help in the relocation of Cubans. The Reverend Agustín Nodal, by then a retired minister, offered consolation and pastoral counseling. The first congregation that held its services in Spanish and that also offered orientations to refugees was begun by this chapter's author and his wife in

Tamiami Methodist Church of Miami on August 1, 1961. In September and October of that year other Spanish-speaking groups were founded in English-speaking congregations in White Temple, Riverside, Wesley, Allappatah, Tarboux, and Grace churches, all of these in Miami.

The work of the Methodist Hispanic-American Church and of the Methodist Latin American Center ended rather suddenly in 1965 when the facilities were confiscated by the state in order to build Interstate Highway 95. The congregation generally dispersed, but a number of faithful members and their pastor, the Reverend Angel Fernández, although disappointed at the loss of their beautiful church, were received by the First Methodist Church of Hialeah—an English-speaking church that was quite distant from their own section of town. Without major Hispanic input in their administration, the funds received from the state's expropriation of the center were reinvested by the church in places and needs that at that time were urgent—for example, the day care centers established by eight congregations over ten years' time and serving more than eight hundred children. The facilities of some churches with Hispanic congregations, such as those in Hialeah and Tamiami, were also improved, and at a later time the creation and operation of Fuster Day School were supported (although the school is now closed because its cost was too high).

At present there are Hispanic congregations of various sizes and in different stages of organization in seven of the fourteen districts in the Florida Annual Conference.

The only Hispanic congregation in the Southeastern Jurisdiction outside of Florida is in Atlanta. It has been almost always served by students in Candler School of Theology, Emory University. It began in 1976 with the work of the Reverend Emilio E. Muller, who was then a student. The Cortés family and sister Carmen Broome are among the founders of this congregation. They have in their midst the presence and the collaboration of the Reverend Dr. Petronila C. Reyes, a retired minister of the Conferences of Cuba and Puerto Rico. They meet in a chapel belonging to St. Mark United Methodist Church.

ORGANIZATIONAL AND STRUCTURAL DEVELOPMENT

The forms that the work among Hispanics in the Southwest has taken show an evolving structure. Reports to Annual Conference, such as those in 1884 and 1887, which have already been mentioned, are not very explicit. The first extensive report was presented by H. B. Someillán to the Annual Conference of 1884, and it dealt with the Cuban Mission in Key West and Havana. With a budget of only $435, one marvels at the prosperity of the mission.

Until the Annual Conference of 1913, appointments were grouped under the title "Cuban Hispanic Mission" (Key West, Tampa, and Cuba). A step forward in acknowledging the importance of this work is to be found in the Acts of 1914 with the creation of the Latin District of Florida, with its own presiding elder and including Key West, Tampa, and Cuba, as well as several Italian congregations. This Latin District was dissolved in 1939, and its congregations, which were by then fewer, were incorporated into their respective geographical districts.

The next twenty years included World War II and the postwar time, which brought profound changes in society at large. Hispanic work also went through a period of transition, which reduced it to three charges: San Salvador in Key West, the Hispanic American Church in Miami, and San Marcos in Ybor City.

This situation changed unexpectedly beginning in 1959 with the arrival of Cuban exiles in unprecedented numbers. By 1966 the new congregations, welcomed by English-speaking churches, were ten in number. Their membership was constantly changing due to the programs of relocation in other cities, sponsored by the Methodist Committee on Overseas Relief and Church World Service.

The resettled Cuban Methodists, along with the rest of the émigré Cuban population, were obsessed by the dream of returning to Cuba soon. This made long-range planning impossible. The emphasis was on social and spiritual services. In

1965 the Reverend J. Lloyd Knox, a former missionary to Cuba and Argentina (elected bishop in 1984), was appointed to advise the Annual Conference's cabinet on Hispanic matters and to promote the interest and support of churches in the Conference for Hispanic work. In 1973 this structure was changed by the creation of a coordinating committee formed by four Hispanic pastors, but with very limited functions in regard to program and administration. Finally, under the direction and leadership of Bishop Joel D. McDavid, in 1975, this committee was organized to become a "Hispanic Committee on Ministry," formed by all Hispanic pastors, a lay delegate from each congregation, two non-Hispanic pastors, two district superintendents, and a representative of the missions area of the Conference Council on Ministries. Its administrative responsibilities are practically nil, and there is only a small budget for a number of Hispanic programs. It publishes a newsletter called *Metohispano*. The Committee has served as a forum for Strategy Consultations in 1975 and 1986 and has also been a channel for the missional emphasis on ethnic minorities and for the work of the Commission on Religion and Race. A number of Hispanic leaders declared in the Strategy Consultation of September 1986 that this structure needs to be redefined and invested with an authority and power that it does not presently have.

Local structures have also followed their own evolution. Hispanic churches have moved from being Hispanic groups within Anglo congregations, with pastors who were appointed as associates and who for some time were members of the Cuba Annual Conference (now an autonomous Methodist Church), to become independent pastoral charges. Their pastors are now members of the Florida Annual Conference. However, the fact that they still share facilities with their mother Anglo congregations (except for three that have their own facilities) creates a number of problems. There still remains on the part of the Anglo congregations a certain well-intentioned paternalism. Mainly for these reasons, southeastern Methodism's outreach to Hispanics lags behind that of other denominations.

LEADERSHIP

The first pastors of Hispanic churches in Florida came out of the congregations themselves. Some of them were highly educated, although most lacked formal training in theology and pastoral administration beyond the Conference Course of Studies of that time. At a later time, the church in Cuba provided almost all the Hispanic ministerial leadership. At present, with two exceptions, all the pastors come from the former Cuba Annual Conference or its successor, the Methodist Church of Cuba, and they are graduates of seminaries in Cuba, Puerto Rico, and the United States. Their average age is fifty-two years. There is only one student in seminary. The only ordained woman transferred to the North New Jersey Conference. There are presently two women candidates to the diaconal ministry. In the Miami District there are also three women who are studying in the Conference Course of Studies at Garrett-Evangelical, preparing for Hispanic work. There is no systematic plan to encourage Christian vocations. At present and in the immediate future, Florida will have to continue importing its Hispanic ministers from other Conferences or from Latin America.

The local congregations were almost the only area in which Hispanic lay people were able to express their leadership, and they are responsible for ensuring continuity in their congregations' work in spite of the irregularity of pastoral services. As the number of Hispanic congregations has increased, the sphere of connectional activities has also widened, and now there are lay Hispanic people present in boards and Conference committees; in 1987 sixteen of them were delegates to Annual Conference. In 1984 a Hispanic delegate represented the Annual Conference in the General Conference, and by 1988 a Hispanic laywoman and two laymen served in that capacity. There are also Florida-based Hispanic members of the General Commission on Religion and Race and of the General Boards of Publications and of Global Ministries.

There is a well-educated, bicultural, and bilingual younger generation in the area that has been preserved from the evils and

102

vices of contemporary society and that is producing a growing number of professionals and university graduates who improve the image of the church and serve the community at large.

The work of United Methodist Women deserves an entire history, not just the short mention that they can be given here. In the case of Florida the Women's Societies were not improvised, for they simply continued the traditions that they brought from Cuba. There is no other sector of Hispanic work in the area that has the activities and connectional participation at the District, Conference, and National level that women have. However, the Hispanic Methodist men have shown increasing participation and leadership in local congregations, and two groups of United Methodist Men have been organized.

GENERAL CHARACTERISTICS

Any doctrinal or theological description of Hispanic United Methodists in the Southeast has to be very general. While both ministers and lay people are open to social and political innovations, and they adapt to the United States in an easy and progressive manner, in their theology and religious practices they reflect a certain tempered pietism, without ascetic exaggerations although with an emphasis on abstinence from tobacco and alcohol and a rejection of lotteries and games of chance. In essence, the religious attitude of Hispanic Methodists follows the Wesleyan tradition that was taught by missionaries and pioneer ministers in their lands of origin. Their preaching is "evangelical," as that term is understood in the United States. They are conservative in their interpretation of Scripture, without fundamentalist extremism, and they are tolerant of pluralistic expressions. The Pentecostal and charismatic movements have not found many followers among the Hispanic Methodists of the region, although the personal sympathy of some pastors for these movements has been felt in their congregations. Also, liberation theology is not well received by the vast majority in this community, who have been traumatized by their political experiences in Cuba and Central America. Hispanic Methodists from Florida frequently react strongly to the political pronouncements and programs of general agencies of The United Methodist Church.

There are no precise statistics concerning Hispanic Protestants in Florida. Probably Methodist numbers are among the most trustworthy, thanks to our careful records. The last estimate of Protestants (December 1983) included 195 organized congregations, 23 missions, and several other groups, making a total of 227 groups with 20,078 baptized members, all of this in Dade County alone. In a study done by the Methodists in 1968, there were only 53 organized Hispanic congregations, with a total of 5,379 members. In less than 20 years the numbers have tripled in both categories. In general, the Baptists have the highest rate of growth. The Catholics are still the majority in a nominal sense, since there is among them a religious syncretism, including people who follow santería, spiritualism, and astrology. Methodist participation in ecumenical programs, as far as Florida Hispanics is concerned, is practically nil.

RECENT DEVELOPMENTS OF NOTE

In the last decades, a number of developments have widened the ministry of Hispanic United Methodists in Florida. One of these is the radio program "New Life in Christ," begun sixteen years ago by Dr. C. D. Stewart, a former missionary to Cuba, and by Mr. Angel Gómez-Tejera. It now continues under the sponsorship of the Miami District under the responsibility of the Reverend Ernesto Vasseur and his wife. This weekly program is broadcast by two stations in Florida and by thirteen others in various Latin American countries.

The Alfalit program, born out of the concern of the Methodist Women of Florida for the literacy of Hispanics, was begun in 1959 under the leadership of Justo González, Sr., and his wife, Dr. Luisa G. González. After moving to Costa Rica, this became an international program serving most of the peoples of Central and South America.

Finally, *Metohispano* is a quarterly publication of the Hispanic Council on Ministries. In its six years of publication it has achieved a good reputation through it excellent typographical presentation and literary content. It is under the direction of the young layman Francisco Montes.

A LOOK TO THE FUTURE

It is difficult to predict the future of Hispanic Methodism in this region. There are too many variables, and the intervening factors are imponderable. Traditional strategies are not always adequate in a population whose very identity is in transition. Immigration has not slowed down and is likely to continue for quite some time. One sometimes has the feeling that the work is forever beginning anew; the mindset of exiles and newcomers hinders their having any sense of permanence.

The generation gap is not yet an acute problem in our congregations, but everything points in that direction. The new generations will have to produce their own ministers and leaders, as the problems of language and identity will continue indefinitely.

5

THE NORTHEASTERN JURISDICTION

Alfredo Cotto-Thorner

Mostly due to the lack of economic opportunities in their countries of origin, thousands of Hispanic Americans have come to this nation in recent years. Most of those coming to the Northeastern Jurisdiction have come from Puerto Rico. During World War I there was a shortage of labor in both factories and farms. In 1917, in order to respond to this situation, Congress approved the Jones Act, which declared Puerto Ricans to be American citizens. In any case, Puerto Rican immigration between 1910 and 1920 was very slow, and the census of 1920 reveals that there were only 11,811 Puerto Ricans in the United States. Most of these were living in New York City, and therefore for the first time there was a Hispanic community in that city. However, during World War II Hispanic immigration grew at an astonishing pace. By then this immigration included not only Puerto Ricans but also people from various Latin American countries. Soon others settled in various areas of the jurisdiction, such as Philadelphia, Boston, Hartford, and Camden. Today there are Hispanics in practically every section of the jurisdiction. These Hispanics retain their national traditions and at the same time make use of the opportunities offered here for their cultural, spiritual, and material development.

Making good use of this opportunity, the missionary agencies of practically all denominations have taken steps to open churches and preaching stations among Hispanics. This is true not only of more traditional denominations such as Presbyterians, Methodists, Baptists, Lutherans, and Disciples of Christ but also of a number of Pentecostal groups, such as the Assemblies of God, which have been able to establish very strong Hispanic congregations. It is estimated that there are in New York City more than five hundred Hispanic churches, several of them with more than a thousand active members.

In contrast, The United Methodist Church has been rather slow in its response to the challenge of work with Hispanics in this jurisdiction. Even though Hispanics have increased rapidly, the Methodist Church did not take steps to establish work among them, as did the Baptists and Presbyterians. New York Conference had its first Hispanic congregation by 1893; Northern New Jersey, by 1954; Southern New Jersey, by 1958; Southern New England, by 1968; Central Pennsylvania, by 1979. Western Pennsylvania did not have its first Hispanic congregation until 1981. I have been unable to trace exact information regarding the beginning of Hispanic work in the remaining Conferences of the jurisdiction.

What follows is an outline of the history of Hispanic Methodism in a number of these Conferences.

NEW YORK CONFERENCE

The Beginnings and Early Years (up to 1960)

In his book *The History of Ethnic Ministries in the New York Conference: The United Methodist Church,* Dr. Henry C. Whyman tells us that in 1892 Mr. Clemente A. Mayo arrived at New York from Mexico in order to "preach the gospel to the Hispanic people of New York." Shortly after his arrival he began preaching in Spanish in Washington Square Church in New York City as well as in the historic church of Sands Street in Brooklyn. The first Hispanic Methodist congregation was organized in Brooklyn, being housed in the Sands Street Church, on January 10, 1893, with nine active members and thirty-five probationary members.

The Reverend Alberto B. Báez, also Mexican, arrived at this city in September 1917 and shortly thereafter was invited to preach to a group of Hispanic Americans who were meeting in Brooklyn. Most likely, this was the same group that Mr. Mayo had earlier gathered and organized. Báez was a product of the missionary work of the Methodist Church in Mexico. It was there that he pursued his theological studies and wed Ms. Thalia Valderrama. The two of them worked as volunteers for a number of years with the congregation of Sands Street. In 1920 he was appointed pastor of that congregation by the Long Island Church Society, and he continued in that position until he retired in 1961. Both the Reverend Báez and his wife had ample missionary vision, and the work they established has served as the base for the creation of other Hispanic congregations in the city.

The second Hispanic congregation to be organized was First Hispanic United Methodist Church in Manhattan. There is very little reliable information regarding its beginnings, but apparently three Hispanics gathered in a home on May 28, 1922, and decided to continue holding services in Spanish. Later, as their numbers grew, they moved to the Metropolitan Temple on Seventh Avenue. Their first pastor was the Reverend Ferdinand B. Aparicio, who for several years was an advocate for Hispanics settling in the city.

Some years later, Mr. Diego Flores, a lay member and local preacher of that congregation, was appointed its pastor. Under his leadership the church developed greatly, becoming the largest Hispanic congregation in the city at the time. It was also during that period that the church building where the congregation gathered, on the corner of 111 Street and Lexington Avenue, was destroyed by fire. With the help of the Methodist City Society, the congregation was able to rebuild on the same site and to this day continues serving the Hispanic community through a day care center and several other social programs.

South Third Street United Methodist Church was the third Hispanic Methodist congregation to be organized in the city. In 1938 the Reverend Agustín Alvira arrived from Puerto Rico, after having worked there for several years. His purpose was to spend some leisure time in New York, in order then to return to Puerto Rico to continue serving as a pastor. However, the opportunity that existed to preach the gospel to the Hispanic people in Brooklyn was great, and he therefore began gathering with other Hispanics in the home of sister Mary Torres, celebrating weekly meetings for prayer and Bible study. Later, at the invitation of the Reverend Timothy Peshkoff, who was then pastor of South Third Street Methodist Church, Alvira and the Hispanic group began meeting in that location. This was then the only Hispanic congregation in the neighborhood. Alvira managed to build a large congregation, and in 1947 he resigned from that position in order to become a pastor to another congregation in the Bronx. At that point the Reverend Antonio Fernández, ex-Catholic priest, was appointed pastor of the congregation in South Third. He was expecting that his ordination as a priest in the Catholic church would be acknowledged by the Methodist Church. When he discovered that this would not be the case, he resigned from this position and accepted a pastorate with a nearby Episcopal Church. All the congregation left with him, with the exception of six people. Given that situation, the Reverend A. Cotto-Thorner (the author of this chapter), a Baptist pastor who is also a social worker, was invited to serve there during weekends for "two or three weeks," while a good Methodist pastor could be found. This was in 1949, and the author remained in that church until he retired in 1988. Thanks to his experience as a social worker, his congregation was noted for its social services to the community.

During the ensuing years other Hispanic congregations were organized, among them Grace, Jefferson Park, Long Island City, Elton Avenue (in the Bronx), and Corona. This last church was founded by the Reverend Juan Sosa. Although Cuban in origin, Sosa came to New York through San José, Costa Rica. He was there when he received an invitation to be pastor of an independent Protestant church in the Bronx. Shortly after having begun his work there, he persuaded the congregation to join the Methodist Conference. Later, while he was still serving the same church, he organized services in Corona, New York, where there were practically no Hispanic churches of any denomination at the time. From its very beginnings the group in Corona gave proof of its potential, and Sosa was transferred there in order to develop the work. Today this is one of the fastest growing churches in the city. Sosa had no peer in his zeal for organizing new congregations, and through the years God used him to found the following: Elton Methodist Church (1964); St. Stephen in the Bronx (1974); Fordham Road, also in the Bronx (1976); the church in Co-op City (1974); and the church in Yonkers (1984). All of these congregations are presently organized as churches.

Expansion Between 1960 and 1980

Shortly after World War II, thousands of Hispanics began arriving in New York. The churches profited from this situation, and there was general enthusiasm. In 1960 Dr. Henry C. Whyman was appointed executive secretary of the Methodist City Society. For many years this organization has worked throughout the city, organizing churches and programs for all ethnic groups. Given the number of Hispanics who were arriving at the time and Dr. Whyman's missionary interests, Methodist Hispanic work began a period of greater development. This was also the time when, due to political problems in Cuba, several Cuban pastors came to New York, and they made a significant contribution with their experience, gifts, and devotion to the expansion of the work. We were later blessed by receiving a group of equally devoted Dominican pastors. There have also been in New York pastors from Argentina, Mexico, Colombia, and Central America. However, from the very beginning and throughout all its history, most of the pastors who have come to serve in New York Conference as well as in the rest of the jurisdiction have come from Puerto Rico. Also, in more recent years our congregations have produced candidates for ordained ministry who now occupy pastoral and administrative positions. The number of those called to ministry has increased in recent times, and now we have men and women who are training in seminary in order to be able to work in Hispanic churches.

Until 1965 our Conference had not ordained any Hispanic

women. It was in that year that Dr. Noemí Díaz, who had arrived from Cuba years earlier with a doctorate in law, was received into the Conference. Dr. Díaz served as pastor to the Church of All Nations for over twenty years, until her retirement. She was also a leader in the Methodist Women's Movement in the city. After that date, several women were ordained, and now there are several studying in colleges and seminaries with the ordained ministry as a goal.

The contribution of lay people has also been important. The Methodist Hispanic Women's Association was organized under the leadership of Dr. Noemí Díaz and Mrs. Milagros Morgado, who from the very beginning had the support of Hispanic Methodist women. This organization has always been mission minded and has helped train women for work in their own congregations. At the same time Dr. Edmundo Morgado, with the help of Mr. Nicasio Díaz, founded the Hispanic Methodist Men's Association. This group worked actively for several years. Besides Mr. Díaz, Drs. Morgado and Humberto Carrazana were noteworthy for their work in leadership training. Thanks to their work, and to those who continued it, every summer the Hispanic Methodist people have the opportunity to participate in camps, and it is there that many young people from our churches have been called to serve the Lord in the ordained ministry.

It was also at this time that Hispanic Methodists in New York began to participate in the national activities of the church. The Reverend Josué Rosado and the author were elected to be part of the steering committee of the National Hispanic Caucus (MARCHA). Since that time, Hispanic leaders of the jurisdiction have been participants in this caucus. In 1971 the New York Conference elected its first Hispanic delegates to General Conference, Mr. Ramón Aponte and the author.

The Hispanic work of the New York Conference is not limited to the five boroughs of the city of New York but extends also to several places in Long Island and Connecticut, as well as into upstate New York. The work in Connecticut began in 1973 and has taken place in Norwalk, New Haven, Bridgeport, Waterbury, and Stamford. The Bridgeport congregation has grown the most of all of these.

Development Since 1980

With the appointment in 1980 of the Reverend Pedro P. Pirón as coordinator of Hispanic Methodist work in New York, we began a stage of growth and expansion. Until that time, Hispanic United Methodists in New York had been as rudderless ships, each going in its own direction. Through pastoral retreats, visits to congregations, and his own particular gift to serve as a bridge between Hispanics and Anglos, Pirón soon obtained good results. During the two years in which he served as coordinator, new work was begun in several sites. However, given the manner in which the Hispanic program itself had been structured, the coordinator had very little freedom. In that difficult situation, Pirón felt that he should resign. But he had already established the guidelines and the direction Hispanic work should follow. On the recommendation of the Hispanic Caucus in 1983, the Reverend Dilca Lebrón, was appointed to take Pirón's place, which she also held for two years. In 1985 the Reverend Héctor Navas, a member of the Conference who had being serving as a missionary in Argentina, was appointed associate program director of the New York Conference. Among his responsibilities was Hispanic work. With this appointment, that work and its leaders lost their struggle to have a full-time coordinator.

At present the New York Conference has twenty-four Hispanic congregations. Some of these are located in the poorest areas. Others are in middle-class areas that have large numbers of Hispanics. Some of the latter, such as Corona in Queens and the church in Co-op in the Bronx, are practically self-supporting.

NEW JERSEY

For a long time, Hispanics arriving in the Northeast would settle in the metropolitan area. But as time went by the Hispanic population expanded to other areas.

By 1953 there were in Camden, New Jersey, between six and seven thousand Hispanics. Most of these were Puerto Ricans with a Catholic heritage. But until that time there was not even a Catholic congregation there for Hispanics, much less a Protestant one. It was then that the Reverend Benjamin F. Allgood, president of the Board of Missions of the New Jersey Conference, made a study of the Hispanic community in Camden, in order to determine if it was necessary to begin Hispanic work there. The bishops of the New Jersey Conference and of the Puerto Rico Conference were very much impressed with the results of this study and decided to open Methodist work in that city as soon as possible. In 1954 a committee of pastors from New Jersey visited the Annual Conference of Puerto Rico, and shortly thereafter they invited the first pastor to begin this work. After many vicissitudes, changes in leadership, and moving their meeting place, by 1979 this congregation was invited to take possession of an old church that was vacant. Finally, in 1981, it was formally organized as a church. Then, in 1983, it merged with another that had also been organized in Camden.

In several other areas of New Jersey the Hispanic community has grown and offered the opportunity for the establishment of Hispanic ministries. In 1953 the Board of Missions of the South New Jersey Conference made a study of the ethnic population within its territory and became aware of the growth in the Puerto Rican population and the possibility of beginning ministry with them. At that time a Methodist family from Utuado, Puerto Rico, was also feeling the need to gather with others for worship. Thus began the idea of establishing Hispanic Methodism in Trenton. That year, a young Puerto Rican engineering student, Agripino Pérez, began visitation work in the area. Due to his college obligations he could not continue, but Mr. Neftalí Maldonado, a young member of the congregation, took up his responsibilities. In 1959 the Reverend Ceferino Lugo was appointed the first pastor of that congregation. There were eighteen people present in his first service. He died in 1962, and the Reverend Emilio Chaviano was appointed as interim pastor.

This work was located in Central Methodist Church, and in

1963 the Reverend Julio Gómez was appointed as Hispanic minister of that congregation. This was formally organized as a church in 1972. Under Gómez's leadership, this congregation has been helping in the cultural and social development of the Hispanic community, offering such programs as music lessons and various forms of orientation for adults. It has also established lay worker institutes and has served the community in a number of other ways. It presently has seventy-five members.

During the 1960s, several other congregations were founded. The first was founded in 1965 in Keyport by the Reverend Francisco Sanfiel, who had recently arrived from Cuba. At the beginning 99 percent of the members of this congregation were Puerto Ricans. Now the congregation includes Argentineans, Hondurans, Chileans, Uruguayans, Dominicans, Spaniards, and Puerto Ricans.

Hispanic work in Lakewood was begun at the insistence of the Anglo church there. Later this work grew with the arrival of vast numbers of Central Americans leaving their countries because of the political convulsions there. The church actually has forty active members, and about 115 families are involved in its programs. The membership roll of Hispanics and Anglos is kept together. Hispanic children attend Sunday school in English, and worship services in Spanish are held on Sunday afternoons. This Hispanic congregation has independence as its main goal.

In 1986, at the invitation of the Anglo congregation in Vineland, the Reverend Nelson Arroyo was appointed to begin Hispanic work there and also to serve the Anglo congregation.

At present there are in the Southern New Jersey Conference only three organized Hispanic churches and a Hispanic congregation that is part of an Anglo one. In 1983 the Conference approved a plan for six Hispanic ordained ministers, for new ministries.

On April 24, 1977, the Hispanic congregations gathered together for the first time in order to organize a Hispanic caucus. There were representatives of the congregations in Trenton, Camden, and Lakewood; Keyport did not attend. The Reverend Julio Gómez was appointed president. In 1982 the caucus gathered again and approved a formal constitution. In 1983 the four Hispanic congregations joined the national Methodist Hispanic caucus (MARCHA). Gómez was the first executive director of this caucus.

EASTERN PENNSYLVANIA CONFERENCE

Hispanic work began in Philadelphia about thirty years ago. The Reverend Josafat Curti was the first pastor of the Church of El Mesías, which gathered in the facilities of Spring Garden United Methodist Church. Later the Reverend Flor Reina and the Reverend Efraín Cotto, Jr., succeeded him. When an Anglo church building became vacant, it was given to El Mesías. This church, with its pastor Cotto, served as the resource for beginning another one in the southern area of Philadelphia.

Another Hispanic church was organized in Philadelphia under the leadership of the Reverend Moisés Freytes. It gathered in a church building belonging to an Anglo congregation on Erie Avenue, and later in another in Hunting Park. After some time, the Hispanic congregation became the sole user of the facilities in Hunting Park and of the parsonage that went with them.

The Hispanic church in Lancaster began by gathering in the Anglo church of Saint Paul some twenty years ago. After moving twice to the facilities of other English-speaking churches, they rented a house in which to meet, and finally, under the leadership of the Reverend Milca Plaud and the Reverend Irving Cotto, they built their own church building. This was dedicated on May 5, 1985. Lancaster was the first Hispanic church in the area to buy its own lot and build its own facilities.

The work in Kenneth Square began under the leadership of the Reverend Victoria Martínez, who went to that community in order to pursue studies beyond those in which she was already involved in seminary. Martínez found that there were a large number of Hispanics in the area, and that there was need for a United Methodist church. This challenge was presented to the Annual Conference, and evangelistic and social work was begun in

1978. A group was organized, which began meeting in an Episcopal church, since there was no Methodist church in the area. This is a community formed mostly by Mexican laborers who work in mushroom farms. In 1984, with the economic help of the Westchester District, the United Methodist church Cristo Rey bought a property that could serve as its gathering place.

As part of a joint program between Puerto Rico and the Eastern Pennsylvania Conference, Irving Cotto came to New York to study in 1977. He was appointed to work in Reading, Pennsylvania, in order to explore the possibility of beginning a Hispanic Methodist church there. With the help of Central United Methodist Church in Reading, Cotto began that ministry. There was a program of tutoring for schoolchildren that was financially supported by the Conference Commission on Religion and Race. There was also a weekly television program in Spanish, "El Nuevo Horizonte." Finally, this congregation was organized as a pastoral charge.

Hispanic work began in Allentown on the basis of the interest of Trinity United Methodist Church in offering a ministry to the children of the Hispanic community that surrounds it. Occasionally, pastors from other Hispanic churches in the Conference would go to Allentown to share with the children and their parents, offering them music and worship services. A summer program was established that included fairs, picnics, music, and other lively activities. As the group grew, it became apparent that a pastor was needed for that ministry. The Reverend Francisco Franceschi and his family were brought to Allentown from Puerto Rico. The group was then organized as a church, which continued growing and eventually acquired a property in which it provides educational services to the community.

OTHER CONFERENCES IN THE JURISDICTION

Hispanic work began in the Western New York Conference through the efforts of Emmanuel United Methodist Church in Rochester. The administrative board of that church, taking note of the racial change in its community, decided to seek ways to serve the new residents. Several attempts were made to begin this work by using Pentecostal lay leaders and then people from the Teen Challenge program. However, these approaches did not succeed. Finally, in 1979, the Reverend Ramón A. Evangelista was transferred from the New York Conference to the Western New York Conference in order to make a study of the possibilities of Hispanic work in the Rochester area. The first service took place in the spring of 1980. The attitude of the English-speaking congregation was very positive; eventually it left its building and even its savings account to the Hispanic church.

In the Western New York Conference there are presently two Hispanic churches, one in Rochester and another in Buffalo. Average attendance is thirty in Rochester and seventy in Buffalo. The Rochester congregation is 90 percent Puerto Rican and 10 percent Dominican. The one in Buffalo is entirely Puerto Rican.

In other areas, The United Methodist Church has not had great success among Hispanics. In the Southern New England Conference there are only three Hispanic congregations. Western Pennsylvania Conference and Central Pennsylvania Conference each have one Hispanic church. The average attendance in most of these churches is barely fifty.

UNITED EFFORTS

For a number of years a group of pastors and laity from several Conferences, especially Northern New Jersey and New York, gathered in order to discuss the need for a Hispanic jurisdictional organization that would give the Hispanic church a sense of direction. In October 1981, at Grace United Methodist Church in New York, an assembly of all the Hispanic pastors of the jurisdiction and four lay persons from each local church took place. These gathered with the purpose of creating such a jursdictional organization, and of discussing the future of the Hispanic church. This was the origin of the Methodist Hispanic Association of the Northeastern Jurisdiction. In January 1984 this association, represented by its president the Reverend Víctor Bonilla and by treasurer the Reverend Jeremías Rojas, met in Puerto Rico with the College of Bishops of the Northeastern Jurisdiction in order to present a document of projections for the Hispanic church.

At present this association is studying the opening of a Biblical Institute of Christian Formation for Laity. This institute will be divided into nine centers of study throughout the jurisdiction. The association has placed this project under the care of the associate director of the Multi-Ethnic Center in Madison, New Jersey, the Reverend Lydia Lebrón-Johansen.

From its inception, MARCHA found support in the Hispanic groups of the New York Conference and the two Conferences in New Jersey. Although MARCHA has had little direct influence in the local congregations, it has made an impact by creating projects and plans for the development of the work. One of the most important contribution of MARCHA in the jurisdiction has been its continuing help and support to Hispanic students.

SOCIAL PROGRAMS

Most of our churches are placed in areas with deep social problems, and they must respond to this need. Unfortunately, very few congregations have been able to establish such programs, due to the lack of funds and personnel. However, several can be mentioned:

1. Anchor House is a rehabilitation center for drug and alcohol addicts that is housed in the United Methodist church of Sur Tres. It is only for men and has facilities for twenty-two residents.
2. At the United Methodist church in Astoria, Long Island City, there is an orientation center specializing in helping undocumented persons, which responds to requests from all over the city.

3. In the United Methodist church in Corona there is a center for seniors.
4. In the same church there is also a program for preschool children.
5. The United Methodist church of Sur Tres has a telephone ministry, "Su Amigo," that counsels and helps people who call requesting spiritual help.
6. In the United Methodist Church of Trenton there is a music school that provides instruction in playing several sorts of instruments.

GENERAL CONSIDERATIONS

In almost every place where work has begun, the laity have been the first to acknowledge the need for the establishment of a congregation. Their zeal and love for the development of the work are the inspiration that has moved the pastors to continue forward even when circumstances have been adverse.

It was not until 1961 that the first United Methodist woman pastor, Dr. Noemí Díaz, was received as an elder in full connection in the New York Conference. As she herself asserts, it was very difficult for her to attain this, since she had to face very strong opposition. With her appointment a new era began in The United Methodist Church, which has been a great blessing for the church in general. In 1987 there were only six Hispanic women pastors in our jurisdiction. There were also several studying in seminaries.

A factor that has delayed the progress of Hispanic work is that most of our churches are in the poorest areas of their cities. This has created in these congregations an economic dependency on the Conference that has hindered their assuming greater responsibility for their own support. There are very few Hispanic congregations that can cover their expenses without help from their Conferences. The economic level that the Conference requires for a congregation is at least $40,000 a year, and this only for pastoral support and administrative expenses. The members of our churches are generous with their offerings, but the Methodist system almost forces the churches to continue depending on Conference funds.

In almost all the Conferences of the jurisdiction, a large part of the Hispanic congregations has being organized and meets in churches belonging to English-speaking congregations, with which they share facilities. Many are in situations in which the Anglo congregation looks upon Hispanics as inferior or second-class Christians, and where justice and equality have either been forgotten or are gone with the wind. Fortunately this situation has been improving, and the Hispanic churches in Philadelphia, New Jersey, and New York that are working together with Anglo congregations report that relationships are better at present.

At least as important a factor in the slow development of our congregations is the system of itinerant ministry of The United Methodist Church. Perhaps this was effective when it began many years ago. But today, given the problems of the cities and the manner in which the work has to be done, ministers can only be effective in their congregations if they identify with them, are part of them, and cease thinking that the superintendent or the bishop will send them someplace else. The largest congregations in the jurisdiction are those whose pastors have joined the struggle with the membership and have remained faithful to a place for a number of years. It is clear that in certain cases a transfer is necessary. But the system has been abused, to the detriment of the congregations.

Another of the difficulties in the development of the Hispanic church in this jurisdiction is that we live amidst a people in transition, who always nurture the hope of returning home. For that reason the church grows very slowly. Hispanics, especially Puerto Ricans, are constantly dreaming of the day when they will return to their homes. Sometimes we say that they keep their luggage packed in order to be ready to leave. This creates a situation of constant change in the leadership of the church, and pastors constantly have to begin anew, training new lay leadership.

Year after year the various Conferences include in their budgets significant amounts of money for Hispanic work. However, these funds lack direction and supervision. Hispanic pastors receive no stimulus from their superiors. Hardly one receives a note from executives encouraging the pastor or the family. The Conference expects pastors to produce and at the same time to spend most of their time attending meetings that appear in the calendars of the superintendent or of the Conference.

Another factor that has interrupted our development is the lack of unity among Hispanic ordained leadership. It is true that we all speak the same language, but we express our lives in different ways. Nationalism has divided us for many years, creating problems that have caused deep wounds in our relationships.

Another hindering characteristic is the diversity in the theological outlook within our own Hispanic congregations, which are formed by people who come from different denominations since the high cost of transportation means that people must attend the closest church. Therefore, it is quite common to find in a single congregation Baptists, Presbyterians, Lutherans, Pentecostals, and others, each trying to show that their tradition or their way of doing things is the best.

The vast majority of Hispanic congregations are conservative, by reason of the inheritance that we have brought with us from our own lands. Many of the people who attend our churches were converted in their native countries. The percentage of the people converted in our churches is very low, perhaps because evangelistic zeal has slowly eroded. The result is that although today we have more Hispanic churches than ever before in the metropolitan area of New York, the total number of persons reached by these churches is approximately the same as before.

Hispanic communities are in constant transition. It is on the basis of this that we can understand the dynamic of change in our congregations. When looking at the future of the church one cannot ignore this reality. In the future Hispanic Methodism will continue being a process of transition. Whatever happens in Latin America will have its effects in this country. New groups of immigrants will continue arriving no matter what the laws of immigration might say. Most of the Hispanics who now reside here will remain here. It is expected that by the year 2000, when we reach the fourth or fifth generation, our people will speak more English and therefore our congregations will have to be bilingual.

With the demise of the missional priority, the model of mission financed by the ecclesiastical structure will be greatly affected. This will imply new missionary models, or in some cases even no mission at all. But it can also bring about the revitalization and strengthening of the solid churches that may provide a beachhead for a mission coming from the Hispanic church and not from the wider structures of The United Methodist Church.

We also begin to envision the development of a particular theology of Hispanics in this area. In the book of Acts we are told that the disciples were to be witnesses of Jesus "to the ends of the earth." The future is full of uncertitude, difficulties, and challenges. But in spite of all this, the Lord will be with us here in this end of the earth to which we have arrived, so that we may continue being his witnesses wherever we may be. The foundation is laid, and with God's help, Hispanics will not turn back.

6

THE NORTH CENTRAL JURISDICTION

Olga G. Tafolla

It is a known fact that states like Texas, New Mexico, Arizona, and California were once land that belonged to Mexico. In the end the United States took control over all these lands, but Hispanic people who were already there continued to live in those parts. Additionally, people from Mexico were continually coming and going. The Treaty of Guadalupe-Hidalgo in 1848 separated Mexico and the United States politically but not culturally, and crossing back and forth without regard for the new border was a common and constant practice.

What does all this have to do with the development of Methodism among the Hispanic people of the North Central Jurisdiction? Simply that Mexican people were moving toward this part of the country around the era of the fabulous 1920s. This was a time in the history of the United States when our country was experiencing for the first time such things as air mail service. Lindbergh had taken off from Long Island, New York, and made a solo flight to Europe, thus proving that air transportation was truly possible, and the world was suddenly smaller. But it was also the period during which the stock market collapsed, causing full-scale confusion, and people all over the country were struggling for survival. Jobs were suddenly not to be had. Mexican people found themselves right in the middle of this calamity. Mexican harvest workers in the Southwest, where employment was no longer available, were hearing of harvest work opportunities in the Midwest. Some began to migrate to states such as Illinois, Indiana, Iowa, and Michigan.

Many began to stay in these areas and to form their own communities or barrios. This was very evident in Chicago, where in the 1920s there were over a thousand Mexicans in the Chicago metropolitan area alone.

A great number of Mexican people began to come to the Midwest during World War II. Many of these people had friends and families who had established themselves in the Midwest. Consequently, once they were in the United States, they would make their way toward that part of the country. Striving for a better way of living, many were able to find jobs in the urban area of cities such as Chicago, Cleveland, and Detroit. At the end of World War II there were a large number of Puerto Ricans beginning to move into this part of the Midwest, as they sought jobs and an opportunity to enhance their education. The trend continued through the years, and in the 1960s the census indicated that well over 55,000 Hispanics were living in the area of metropolitan Chicago.

Today the population of Mexican Americans, whether they be first-generation, second-generation, or Chicanos of older roots in the United States, is over half a million in Chicago alone. There are also a quarter million Puerto Ricans and another quarter million other Hispanics. This amounts to a total of over a million Hispanics living in the Chicago area. Other areas of the Midwest that include substantial numbers of Hispanics are Detroit and other Michigan cities, Cleveland, Milwaukee, Minneapolis, and Indianapolis.

The data given above provide the outline of a history of the presence of the Hispanic people in the North Central area of our country. With this background well in mind, let us now see where the first Methodist work took place.

It was 1926 when Methodist work among Mexican people first began in the city of Chicago. Ironically, the first church building to house a Hispanic congregation was an Italian Methodist church, which was purchased from them for the sum of one dollar.

This church was known as the Italian Church of the Good Shepherd, so it became the Mexican Iglesia del Buen Pastor.

Bernard O'Neal, who at that point in time was a young man studying at the University of Chicago, was given the task of working among the Mexican people living in that area. Studying and working to build up a new congregation was no easy task. But O'Neal was a determined young man, and the challenge before him must have been intriguing. He succeeded in building up the membership of what became the fastest-growing church of that time. His hard work and dedication earned him the love and respect of that congregation, where he served for twenty years, until 1946.

In the early 1940s a man came from Spain into the United States to serve in the Río Grande Conference, the Reverend Constantino González. He became interested in serving at the Iglesia Del Buen Pastor and succeeded O'Neal in 1946. He loved social work, and under his leadership many social projects were started. He was also a very good preacher. The average attendance on any given Sunday service was well over three hundred. He served the Iglesia Del Buen Pastor for ten years, ending his work there in 1956.

Thus O'Neal and González became the pioneers of Methodist work among the Mexican people in Chicago. These two servants of the Lord definitely left indelible footprints!

The role of the Methodist Church became more intentional and more visible when we became United Methodists. The entire denomination became more aware we were facing changes in our society that were too revolutionary to understand and too controversial to confront. Nevertheless, the black constituency was beginning to become more vocal in demanding dignity, freedom, and justice. The church started to respond to the situation of our black brothers and sisters, and we as Hispanics began to see the need to be involved in the struggles of our brothers and sisters, since we in part faced the same situation. Some Conferences were more intentional than others in their concerns for ethnic persons. The Northern Illinois Conference was one Conference that in the 1960s began to acknowledge the growing number of ethnic persons in its area of service. They created the Missionary Society of Church Extension, whose purpose was to help open storefront ministries.

The storefront ministries became a force among the Hispanic communities. The many small but active churches that are now part of the Northern Illinois Conference are a result of these ministries. These churches not only are meeting the spiritual needs of the people but also are involved in meeting the physical needs of their community. Their programs include day care centers, meals for senior citizens, recreation for children and youth, counseling, and providing information on agencies that can help where the church cannot. They are truly reaching out in love and putting that love to action, remembering the words of Jesus, "inasmuch as you have done it unto one of the least of these my brethren, you have done it unto me."

The Northern Illinois Conference, to confirm the work started with storefront ministries, established missional priorities that provided funding for new areas of work. In 1969, at a special session, this Conference voted to appropriate monies for black people as well as Hispanics. Accordingly, with this kind of support, the Hispanic leadership met and organized La Junta Hispano-Americana. This organization works to develop programs that provide leadership training for both laity and clergy. The allocation given to La Junta in the beginning was $100,000. It is a unique program that has helped Hispanics establish thirteen Hispanic ministries throughout the Northern Illinois Conference, as far as the border of the Iowa Conference. With this kind of support given to both laity and clergy, Hispanic leaders began to be more visible not only in their Conference but also at the jurisdictional level. Their presence at the Jurisdictional Conference gave these leaders the opportunity to advocate for Hispanic concerns. One such concern was that of opening new ministries in other areas of the jurisdiction where there was a concentration of Hispanic persons.

The Junta knew of the many cities in the North Central Jurisdiction where the Hispanic population was heavy and where there were no ministries to meet the spiritual or physical needs of these people. Seeing and hearing of the need for extension of the work started by the Northern Illinois Conference, a special Task Force of Hispanic Leaders was formed. Its job was to do research and to compile data for the different Conferences concerning the needs of Hispanics in the various areas. This research would include surveys and geographic studies detailing information required to determine the need to form new congregations. This project was also supported by the College of Bishops of the Jurisdiction. The surveys and studies performed by the task force resulted in new work in other Conferences.

The Hispanic Task Force has an opportunity to meet with the College of Bishops once every four years to share with them concerns and interests from across the jurisdiction. Such discussion can be of benefit to the Hispanic communities in the various geographical areas these leaders represent. It has been very rewarding to see the fruits of this group's labors. Hispanic ministries have received very good support from their Annual Conferences. Contemporary indication of this support is the fact that the North Central Jurisdictional Conference has allocated funding to the Hispanic Task Force. These monies are used to carry out programs and networking as well to coordinate the concerns of the Hispanic constituency within the North Central Jurisdiction.

One event that has been a great success is the camp-style gathering the Task Force sponsors every year. It is a time during the month of August when pastors and a good number of their congregations come as families to join similar groups from other parts of the jurisdiction. The Task Force is responsible for providing the leadership, and it has been very fortunate to get persons from agencies such as the General Board of Discipleship, the General Board of Higher Education, the General Board of Church and Society, the General Commission on Religion and Race, the General Commission on the Status and Role of Women, and the General Board of Global Ministries. The Task Force has also had leaders come from the Río Grande Conference to help them. These leaders come to be part of the week's event. Their participation is in leading workshops on worship, evangelism,

127

youth programs, and projects. It is through events like this that Hispanics of the North Central Jurisdiction continue to find opportunities for their personal growth and for new insights as to the many resources available. These activities prepare the clergy, as well the laity, to go to their local church and disseminate their knowledge about how The United Methodist Church works. This is particularly beneficial to the local church, since many members come from diverse denominational backgrounds and upbringings.

The story of Hispanic Methodism in the North Central Jurisdiction may date back to 1926, but for many years the Methodist Church was represented only in the Chicago area. In the mid-1950s, through a program called Youth for Christ in Chicago, two young persons responded to the need for new pastors. They sincerely felt called by Christ to dedicate their lives to the work of the church by becoming ministers in the Methodist Church. They left their careers and went to seminaries, one to Asbury Theological Seminary and the other to Garrett Seminary. They came back ready to work among the Hispanic people of Chicago. Soon they became aware that though there was much work for Hispanics in their city, there was also much to do across their Conference and beyond.

Much of what has happened around the Northern Illinois Conference has been through the efforts and leadership of these two persons. They have helped bring in new leaders to the area. Their leadership has been of great value to the Hispanic Task Force, the Hispanic people of the North Central Jurisdiction, and the entire Northern Illinois Conference. Much more could be said about them, but it is sufficient to say that they have touched the lives of many. The young men are now mature persons: the Reverend José Velásquez of Juan Huss United Methodist Church, Chicago, and the Reverend Finees Flores of Albany Park United Methodist Church, also in Chicago. These two have also left indelible footprints!

It is not only in Chicago that United Methodists have worked among Hispanics. Indeed, there are Hispanic churches throughout the Jurisdiction. The story of the founding and early years of the First Hispanic United Methodist Church in Kenosha may serve to illustrate the origin of those churches.

The United Methodist Church began work among Wisconsin's Hispanic population by doing ecumenical work among migrant farmworkers in the 1960s. Then, during the early 1970s, attention was given migrants who had settled in Racine. With the arrival of Ilda and Fred Thomas to Kenosha, the Southeast District shifted its Hispanic focus from Racine to Kenosha. In July 1977, as a part of the ethnic minority church development program of the Wisconsin Conference, Ilda Thomas was asked to survey the communities.

In February 1978 the Southeast Ethnic Ministry (SEEM) was initiated. Using the results of the survey, a program of action was planned, and Ilda Thomas was hired with a salary paid by the Conference Board of Global Ministries. A Hispanic family program was begun at the Christian Youth Council (CYC). Visitation and contacts with community leaders, Hispanic churches, and agencies continued. An ecumenical committee was formed. This committee planned and supervised the activities. The first chairperson was a Catholic deacon. In August 1978, a citywide interdenominational Bible school was held, which became an annual event. During September 1978 the first Hispanic Fair was held in downtown Kenosha. Hispanic churches, agencies, and Anglo and Hispanic people took part in the planning and celebration. This also became an annual event.

During 1979 a Hispanic Board was created, made up of pastors of the four United Methodist churches in Kenosha and a lay representative of each church plus the director of the Christian Youth Council and the Director of Hispanic Ministry. Benel López was hired as staffperson to begin to explore more intentionally the possibility of establishing a Hispanic United Methodist congregation. Bible studies began in homes. One family, the Javier and Paz Aguilar family, showed interest from the very beginning in learning about the church. This family, together with the Mares family, later became the core of the new congregation. On October 5, 1980, the first Hispanic United

Methodist worship service was held. Benel López became the pastor of the new congregation.

In 1981 the Reverend Miguel Arroyo was asked to serve the congregation in the hope that he would become a full-time pastor, since López had asked to be relieved of his responsibilities because of his studies, work, and family obligations. That same year, the Reverend Dick Truitt, the district superintendent, led the service of consecration of the new congregation, which met at Memorial United Methodist Church. Finally, in 1984, this First Hispanic United Methodist Church moved to Immanuel United Methodist Church; a study made by the Reverend Elí Rivera had concluded that Immanuel was a better place to reestablish the church, since there were more Hispanics in that area.

The history of Hispanics and their work in the North Central Jurisdiction is a short journey in terms of the number of years. However, bringing this material together has given us a vivid picture of where we are and how much more there is to do. We see that there are extensive fields ready for harvest.

One of the goals of Hispanics in the North Central Jurisdiction is to work toward the creation of new churches. In fact, they will strive to have forty new churches by the year 2000. It is hoped most of them will be self-supporting.

We dream of congregations rooted in the faith that lived in the pioneer leaders. We are certain they have passed that faith on to men and women who continue to respond to God's call. Hispanics are definitely moving into new roles in the life of The United Methodist Church. They have developed their roots.

We look back and realize the tremendous challenge before us. However, looking back has been good, for we can see the legacy left by our pioneers, a legacy we need to live up to. And with God's help we will!

7

PUERTO RICO

Gildo Sánchez

Beginning in 1898, when the Mission Board of the former Methodist Episcopal Church took its first steps toward missionary entry into Puerto Rico, the historical process of The United Methodist Church in Puerto Rico covers more than ninety years.

The history of the church in Puerto Rico can be divided into five periods: the beginning of the mission, the establishment of the mission, the organization of the Missionary Conference, the Provisional Annual Conference, and the Annual Conference of Puerto Rico. By dividing our history into these five periods it is possible both to outline the main steps in the development of the church and to follow the various organizational alternatives Methodism supplies.

PUERTO RICO TOWARD THE END OF THE NINETEENTH CENTURY

It was in his second voyage, on November 19, 1493, that Christopher Columbus discovered the island of Puerto Rico, which the natives of the area called Borinquen. That was the beginning of a period of Spanish rule that lasted from 1493 to 1898. While under Spanish rule, the island served as a center for the defense of shipments of gold and silver to Spain from the mines in Mexico, Colombia, and Peru. The original inhabitants that Columbus found in Puerto Rico were members of the peaceful tribe of the "taínos." Very early during the process of colonization they were subjected to slavery, then decimated; eventually their place was taken by black Africans who were subject to similar or worse slavery.

The Spanish-American War, which began in the Caribbean region with the sinking of the battleship Maine before the port of Havana, Cuba, in February 1898, also extended to Puerto Rico. A few months later, on July 25, 1898, American troops landed in the southern seaport of Guánica. The skirmishes connected with the invasion lasted only a few weeks, with the result that the flag of Spain was taken down in the main castle, La Fortaleza, in San Juan, and its place was taken by the American flag. The Spanish-American War formally ended with the Treaty of Paris, promulgated on December 10, 1898. Thus the United States assumed control over Puerto Rico. Immediately a military government was organized and civil rights established. These included freedom of worship. Two years latter, when the Congress of the United States enacted the Foraker Act, President William McKinley declared that the island would enjoy a complete separation between church and state and that there would be freedom of religion. Thus Roman Catholicism was disestablished, all financial support from the government to the church was halted, and the Roman Catholic Church of the United States took charge of its counterpart in Puerto Rico.

Socioeconomic conditions on the island were dismal toward the end of the nineteenth century and the beginning of the twentieth. Poverty was rampant. Hurricanes, especially the one that struck on the day of San Ciriaco, August 8, 1899, had devastated the fields and destroyed most of agriculture. There were hundreds of Puerto Ricans who had never slept on a bed or worn a pair of leather shoes, and who hardly had a hammock on which to sleep. Most of the houses in the countryside and in some sections of the cities hardly had any furniture. There were some 300,000 school-age children who had never seen the inside of a school. Education was the patrimony of the rich, and there was widespread illiteracy among adults. Hunger, few opportunities for work, and a very high mortality rate were the rule. This was the Puerto Rico that the first missionaries found when they began their work.

THE BEGINNINGS OF METHODIST WORK

The publicity given by the news media of the United States to the Spanish-American War, and especially the taking of the island of Puerto Rico; the enactment of the Foraker Act, with its religious implications; and the declarations of President William McKinley awakened interest in the missionary agencies of Protestant churches in the United States. The Board of Foreign Missions of the Presbyterian Church took the initiative in seeking an agreement among various boards in order to undertake missionary work in Cuba, Puerto Rico, and the Philippines. On July 13, 1898, a meeting took place in New York that was attended by several missionary agencies, including Methodists, who played an important role in that meeting. According to the *New York Times* of June 21, 1902, in that meeting it was agreed that "it is the duty of Protestantism in the United States to provide these island inhabitants with a purer faith, and that the various boards are to be supported toward those ends."

By the second half of 1898, the secretaries of the Presbyterian, American Baptist, Congregational, and Methodist Episcopal mission boards gathered in New York. Meeting around a large map of Puerto Rico, they prayed that "God would help them so to enter the island of Puerto Rico that there would never be any missionary hostility of any kind in that island" (*Christian Work in Latin America,* 1917). This comity agreement divided the island into four regions, with each board being responsible for one of them. This division was later adjusted in order to make room for the Christian Church (Disciples), the Christian and Missionary Alliance, the United Brethren in Christ, and the Evangelical Lutheran Church. The two largest cities, San Juan and Ponce, remained open to all denominations.

Clearly the work of the Methodist Church in Puerto Rico was

begun under the best ecumenical and interdenominational auspices. This would later be strengthened with the founding of an institution of theological education, the Seminario Evangélico de Puerto Rico; a magazine, *Puerto Rico Evangélico;* and an organization for joint work, the Unión Evangélica, which later would change its name to Federación de Iglesias Evangélicas, still later to Asociación de Iglesias Evangélicas, and finally to Concilio Evangélico de Puerto Rico.

Early in 1899, the Mission Board of the Methodist Episcopal Church sent Bishop William Xavier Ninde and the Reverend A. B. Leonard, who was one of its officers, to visit Cuba and Puerto Rico and to report on the opportunities in those islands. The report was favorable, and, as a result, in November 1899 the establishment of a mission in Puerto Rico was jointly approved, with an allocation of $6,000 for that project. Dr. Charles W. Drees, who was then serving as a missionary in Argentina, was immediately appointed to serve as superintendent for the mission. He arrived at San Juan on March 25, 1900. Since he was fluent in Spanish, he was able to establish initial contact and to be accepted by the general population. He found on his arrival that the Reverend G. B. Benedict, who was at the time on leave of absence from his Annual Conference in the United States, was in charge of general educational work in the cabinet of the American governor. Benedict would prove to be a valuable asset in the early missionary efforts.

The first Methodist Episcopal service took place on March 30, 1900. Two days later, on April 1, the first congregation was organized. This was an English-speaking congregation. Their members were mostly military residents of San Juan. The name of this church, which would later become Union Church, was San Juan First Methodist Episcopal Church.

The first Puerto Rican congregation was founded by Dr. Drees with a group of thirty people on April 8, 1900, and it gathered at 45 Cruz Street in Old San Juan. It would be known as La Santísima Trinidad Methodist Episcopal Church. Four months later it moved to number 18 Sol Street, where a two-story wooden structure was acquired. The bottom floor was used as a meeting place and the upper story as a parsonage. In 1911 another mission superintendent, Dr. Benjamin S. Haywood, bought the adjoining property, which was a solid brick structure. This latter structure remains to this day, and in the place where the original wooden house stood there is now a beautiful Romanesque church built in 1920.

The first missionaries to arrive in Puerto Rico to work with Dr. Drees were the Reverend John Volmer, the Reverend T. M. Hardwood, the Reverend Samuel Culpeper, the Reverend Manuel Andújar, and the Reverend Peter Van Fleet. Other churches founded soon after the first two in San Juan were Puerta de Tierra, Vieques, Guayama, Arecibo, Utuado, Culebra, Camuy, Ponce, Patillas, and Maunabo. Thus when the dynamic Charles W. Drees left in 1905, after five years of intense missionary work, he left behind some fourteen organized churches; several Sunday schools in those churches; the first issue of the official magazine, *El Defensor Cristiano,* with a run of 2,500 copies and under the directorship of Manuel Andújar; the McKinley Free School, which only lasted a few years; the Washington Institute, which has since disappeared; and the G. O. Robinson Home and Industrial School in Santurce, which first would be a home for orphans and then a private school. He had also recruited nine missionaries to open and serve various churches and four Puerto Rican preachers to work as pastors. One should note that the first Puerto Rican pastor was the Reverend Juan Vázquez, who was given this title in 1903 and appointed to the new work in Camuy. Two other names mentioned together with Vázquez are Genaro Cotto and Enrique Cuervos.

THE FIRST ECCLESIAL STRUCTURE

Scarcely one year after the beginning of missionary work, leaders both in the United States and Puerto Rico began considering the organization of a Puerto Rico Mission. This took place on March 7, 1902, in La Santísima Trinidad Church in San Juan. This constitutive session was presided by Bishop John M.

Walden. At the point of its organization, it had seven missionaries, five pastoral charges, 195 members, two sanctuaries valued at $9,400, and two manses with a value of $3,250.

The mission design of this nascent organization is not explained in detail. However, from a number of indications one can conclude, first, that the purpose of the mission was to complete the "quadrilateral Methodist occupation of the island" by adding beyond the preaching centers of San Juan and Arecibo in the north, Vieques toward the east, and Guayama toward the southeast, and by opening work in the cities of Ponce in the south and Aibonito and Utuado in the center of the island. A second point was to work to recruit and train a native ministry; a third, to acquire properties where preaching could take place; and a fourth, to create a periodical for promotion and a strong evangelistic emphasis in order to win Puerto Ricans for Christ.

This ecclesial organization lasted until 1913, and its leader was really Dr. Benjamin Haywood, the second superintendent. Haywood was aggressive in his leadership and had great intellectual and organizational abilities. He served for nine years, after which he left behind thirty-two organized congregations, seven active missionaries, and twenty-five Puerto Rican pastors who were either in charge of churches or helping some of the missionaries. Some ten new concrete structures were put up, as well as twenty-five small chapels built with wood, tin, and straw. It was also during his tenure that the buildings for the orphans' homes in Santurce and Hatillo were built.

This is the period of the teacher-pastors, as many Puerto Rican pastors were called, who besides tending to a small church taught reading and writing to children and adults in remote rural areas. Many of them are still well remembered, such as Ramón Gómez, Juan Curet Ceballos, Pedro Tomás Méndez, Justo P. Santana, and Agustín Boissén. Others who were not teacher-pastors but who were part of that first generation of Puerto Rican pastors include such distinguished names as Jorge Richardson, Cruz Valle Padilla, José Espada Marrero, Juan Orlandi Bairán, Teodomiro Nieves, and Darío Ruiz Martínez. The latter is known as the Prince of the

Puerto Rican Pulpit. Juan Orlandi Bairán was an astounding leader, founder of many of the Conference programs.

THE PUERTO RICO MISSIONARY CONFERENCE

On March 1, 1913, in the Church of La Santísima Trinidad and with Bishop William Burt presiding, the Missionary Conference of Puerto Rico was organized. This was a great step forward in Puerto Rican Methodism. By then there were 3,218 members, several organized churches, and a number of ordained Puerto Rican pastors.

This Missionary Conference lasted twenty-eight years, from 1913 to 1941. The outstanding leader during much of this period was the Reverend Manuel Andújar, a Spaniard who went to the United States when he was still very young and who studied theology at Drew Seminary in Madison, New Jersey. Andújar was part of the missionary personnel of the early days and had the advantage of knowing the language as well as Hispanic culture. When he died in 1929, his ashes were deposited under the Church of La Santísima Trinidad, a church he had served and greatly loved.

Andújar was known for having founded and directed *El Defensor Cristiano*. As its name indicates, this newspaper played the important role of being an instrument of defense against the attacks and open hostility of the Roman Catholic Church. At that time, the Roman Catholic Church was very much opposed to Protestant churches. This newspaper ceased publication in 1917, when it joined with other Protestant publications in order to found the interdenominational magazine, *Puerto Rico Evangélico*.

The period of the Missionary Conference is marked by a steady decrease in the number of missionaries and an increase in the number of Puerto Rican pastors assuming positions of leadership, as well as by the presence of prominent lay people whose role in the deliberations of the Missionary Conference was significant. Some of these pastors began their training at the feet of the missionaries and left the woodshop, the cobbler's bench, the sugar mill, the coffee plantation, or the classroom in order to become ministers. Some, such as Carlos Ortiz, were efficient and faithful but died young. Others, such as Apolinario Cruz Sánchez, José Seguí, and Domingo Marrero, served as missionaries sent to the Dominican Republic by the church in Puerto Rico .

In 1919 the Bible Institute of Hatillo joined other denominational schools in order to found the Seminario Evangélico de Puerto Rico. This school of theology trained a new generation of ministers. It is there that new candidates for ministry went to study, and many older pastors who were in active service went to improve their training.

The contribution of the Robinson Bible Institute in Hatillo deserves special attention, since it was the first attempt to offer a more solid and organized theological education to the new Puerto Rican pastors who were coming up. This Bible Institute developed within the George O. Robinson Industrial Institute and Training School, which was founded in 1910 in Hatillo. This was a home for orphan boys and in 1915 began being used also in order to house candidates for ministry. The first name mentioned as a student in the Bible Institute is José Espada Marrero, who had four fellow students whose names are not given. The Bible Institute was organized by Bishop Wilbur P. Thierkield, who appointed the Reverend J. K. Hubbard as its dean and missionaries Samuel Culpeper and Manuel Andújar as teachers. They divided the subjects among themselves, although most of the teaching was done by Dean Hubbard, who resided in the institution. Culpeper and Andújar traveled to Hatillo weekly or fortnightly in order to hold classes. The curriculum included the following subjects: harmony of the Gospels, introduction to sacred Scripture, general history, church history, homiletics, pastoral work, Sunday school, logic, and systematic theology. Its duration was short, from 1915 to 1919, when it transferred its students to the Seminario Evangélico de Puerto Rico. Its dean, the Reverend J. K. Hubbard, became the Methodist professor of the new seminary.

The ordination of the first five Puerto Rican elders took place in the 1917 session of the Conference. Ordained were Cruz Valle Padilla, Jorge Richardson, Fulgencio Ortiz, Ramón Gómez, and José M. Morales. Also ordained as deacons were Juan Orlandi, Juan Curet, Vicente Rodríguez, and Justo P. Santana.

The preaching of that time was of high quality, since pastors were well trained intellectually and academically. Problems both of the society and the individual were tackled. The Methodist Church became widely known in government as well as in society. There were a number of pastors with ample intellectual training. One of these was Dr. Domingo Marrero Navarro, a Puerto Rican intellectual who became well known as a writer, philosopher, professor, and university chaplain. Others were Félix D. de la Rosa, Tomás Pereles Hernández, and Tomás Rico Soltero.

The last superintendent of the Missionary Conference was Dr. Bruce R. Campbell, a kind but very passive man. He was helpful and friendly. Before becoming the leader of the church in Puerto Rico he had served in Aibonito, Ponce, and La Santísima Trinidad of San Juan.

It is important to remember that in those early years of the twentieth century, and practically until 1940, social, economic, and political conditions in Puerto Rico were precarious. The work of the missionaries had an important component of social and economic improvement, as well as the preaching of the gospel. It was necessary to educate, to feed, to clothe, and constantly to do other works of charity. Puerto Rico was hit by hurricanes and earthquakes that devastated the island. One of the worst was the hurricane that hit on the day of Saint Philip, 1928. Thousands of families were left homeless, roads were washed away, and agriculture was destroyed. The Methodist Church itself suffered the destruction of several of its churches and parsonages. Besides these conditions, the economic depression that hit the United States in 1930 also affected Puerto Rico. The Mission Board in the United States had to cut much of its subsidy to the church in Puerto Rico. Several pastors were left unemployed, and a number of preaching points were abandoned.

THE PUERTO RICO PROVISIONAL
ANNUAL CONFERENCE

The next stage in the development of the church in Puerto Rico began on February 12, 1941, when under the presidency of Bishop Ernest G. Richardson, in the city of Ponce, the Puerto Rico Provisional Annual Conference was formally formed. This new status gave the church in Puerto Rico almost all the powers that the Discipline of the Methodist Church gave to Annual Conferences. This status would last twenty-seven years, until 1968, when the church was organized as a regular Annual Conference.

It was at that time that the first Puerto Rican delegates were sent to General Conference and to the Jurisdictional Conference of the Northeast. It was also during that time, when the Methodist work on the island had already attained a certain level of maturity and able native leadership had developed, that the first Puerto Rican Superintendent for the Provisional Annual Conference was appointed. This took place in 1949, and the person to receive this privilege was Dr. Tomás Rico Soltero.

The appointment of Tomás Rico Soltero was the beginning of a new stage marked by a constant zeal for the extension of the church, the building of new and beautiful churches, and the purchase of physical facilities for Christian Education programs, for the youth program, and for the establishment of parochial schools.

Episcopal supervision during that time was in the hands of two bishops who left an indelible mark on the church. The first was Bishop Charles W. Flint, a man of great intellectual gifts, a profound preacher, and a loving and affable person. It was he who appointed Dr. Rico Soltero as superintendent. The other was Bishop Fred P. Corson, a leader of strong personality who led the Provisional Annual Conference with a strong hand, to the point of being tyrannical. During the sixteen years of his episcopal function, he impressed the same quality on Superintendent Rico Soltero.

As could be expected, a hard leadership such as that of Bishop

Corson also was in measure inclined to excessive paternalism, and this would hinder the maturity and independence of the church. A consequence was that human resources, both lay and pastoral, were not fully used. This can be seen in that for twenty-one years the same person occupied the position of superintendent.

However, the church did grow in membership, new pastoral charges were created, good and beautiful church buildings were erected, and old ones were remodeled. The Corson Conference Center in Mameyes, as well as Corson School in Villa Palmeras, were also the result of this period. The latter institution is now known as Centro-Met and has a program of service to the community.

This period produced a new generation of pastors known as "the generation of the forties and fifties." Among them are Benjamín Santana, Rafael Boissén, Gildo Sánchez, Jorge N. Cintrón, Gerardo López, William Fred Santiago, and Andrés Marrero. All of them had ample intellectual and theological training. Several have been outstanding in university and seminary teaching, in the leadership they have given in seminaries and church agencies, and in their pastorate in important churches, and one as a judge.

There were also a number of lay people who gave their lives to the service of the church. The names of Nicolás Briones Cruz, José Quiñones Vicens, Angel Lahoz, Ana Rosa Goitía and others stand out. One should also mention the Reverend Julia Torres Fernández, an educator from Ponce who from early childhood devoted herself to the service of the church and the community and who eventually was ordained to the ministry. "Julita," as she was lovingly called, studied theology in the Evangelical Seminary and became one of the first women pastors in Puerto Rico. Another woman who became a pastor was the Reverend Dolores Lebrón Andújar.

THE PUERTO RICO ANNUAL CONFERENCE

This stage began on June 26, 1968, when the church was finally organized as an Annual Conference, with Bishop Fred P. Corson presiding. This is the present status of the church. Its episcopal leaders, after Bishop Corson, have been Bishops J. Gordon Howard, from 1968 to 1972; James M. Ault, from 1972 to 1980; F. Herbert Skeete, from 1980 to 1988; and Susan M. Morrison, from 1988 to the present. Bishop Morrison is the first woman to preside in the Puerto Rico Annual Conference. These bishops have worked democratically and effectively. They have also moved toward liberating the church from subjection to a paternalism in which it was expected that all was to be done at the national levels of the church. These bishops, especially Ault and Skeete, have related to the Puerto Rican church at a more personal and intimate level than have any of the previous bishops. They served as enablers of the process of the church toward self-determination. They have opened the way so that Puerto Rican pastors are able to work in Anglo Annual Conferences. There are presently more than twenty-five Puerto Rican pastors serving Hispanic, bilingual, or Anglo churches or serving in general boards and agencies. Likewise, Puerto Rican delegates to General and Jurisdictional Conferences have made a significant contribution. The Annual Conference of Puerto Rico nominated one of its pastors, the Reverend Gildo Sánchez, as a candidate for bishop before the Jurisdictional Conference of the Northeast in 1976 and again in 1980. As was to be expected, at that time there was not sufficient interest in the Northeastern Jurisdiction in electing a Hispanic bishop.

During this stage, the leadership of the church has been in the hands of superintendents Rafael Boissén, from 1965 to 1975; Gildo Sánchez, from 1975 to 1981; Luis F. Sotomayor, from 1981 to 1985; and Myriam Visot, from 1985 to the present. The Reverend Myriam Visot is the first woman superintendent. At other times, and by decision either of the bishop or of the Conference itself, other leaders have served as district superintendents, such as Jorge Richardson, Félix de la Rosa, Juan Orlandi, Apolinario Cruz Sánchez, José A. Robles, Jesús Amaro, Bienvenido Güisao, Angel Arús, and Israel Ramos.

During this time the church has produced many young pastors

142

who are dedicated, well trained, full of enthusiasm, and committed to the church.

A METHODIST PUERTO RICAN CONSCIOUSNESS

During the course of this history a very particular and well-defined Puerto Rican Methodist consciousness has been developing. This is the result of a series of religious, cultural, political, and sociological elements that have come into play during the nine decades of the history of the church. These elements, sometimes unseen and at other times quite evident, have been present in the everyday work of the church. Sometimes they have united it, and sometimes they have polarized it. Sometimes they have delayed its growth, and sometimes they have propelled it forward. Given the importance of these elements, they must be outlined here.

The first is the relationship between the U.S. occupation of the island in 1898 and the beginning of missionary work. Both the mission leadership and the population of the island saw the missionaries as agents of Americanization. At times the people received the missionaries fully because of the social and educational services they offered, but at other times they strongly rejected them, in particular the Roman Catholic sector of the population. The first missionaries had no consciousness of being agents of this Americanizing process, yet they did believe that jointly with the gospel of Jesus Christ they were bringing a form and style of life that would benefit the island. They were importing certain political principles of which they were convinced. The United States also employed the services of missionaries in order to extend those principles and cultural styles through educational programs, social services, and community improvement programs. It suffices to glance at the speeches of political and military leaders in the United States, on the one hand, and of executives of missionary boards, on the other, to prove this point.

The vast majority of early Methodist converts accepted these principles and life-styles, as did the generations of the first three decades. There were times in which practically all the pastors and lay leaders were Republicans, which in Puerto Rico meant that they favored assimilation into the United States. However, the same was true of the vast majority of the population of Puerto Rico, which gladly accepted the citizenship granted to them by means of the Jones Act of 1917. Both the secular Puerto Rican press and the Protestant press welcomed this event. There are two articles praising this achievement of citizenship, written by the Reverend José Espada Marrero and the Reverend Jesús M. Amaro, in one of the issues of *Puerto Rico Evangélico* of that year. On the other hand, there were minority sectors that invoked deeply patriotic feelings in order to reject the Jones Act of 1917, and that continued calling for total separation from the United States. This was vigorously debated in some parties, especially the Liberal Party, and became an absolute emphasis for the Nationalist Party, whose leader was Dr. Pedro Albizu Campos. Among the ranks of Puerto Rican pastors there were several who took a stance, some with the moderate separatism of the Liberal Party and others with the radical separatism of the Nationalist Party. One of the latter was the Reverend Juan Hernández Valle, a Methodist pastor of great charisma, who actively participated in the political campaigns of don Pedro Albizu Campos. As a consequence of his nationalistic involvement, Valle opted for politics, abandoning the ministry and devoting himself to law. In the decade of the 1940s, due to his active political participation and the bloody events of those years, he was arrested and was made to serve a long prison term. In spite of this he is remembered as a good Christian, a good pastor, and a great intellectual.

Luis Muñoz Marín in his early years advocated separatism but then turned toward political autonomy as a formula to solve the grave economic and political problems of Puerto Rico. Without the use of weapons or bloody revolts, he achieved a peaceful revolution through his Popular Democratic Party. He attained power in 1940, and his rule was marked by progress in economic, social, educational, and health matters. His work toward autonomy led to the creation of the Estado Libre Asociado (Commonwealth) of Puerto Rico, in 1952. This defines the relationships between Puerto Rico and the United States in terms of autonomy, with greater clarity and precision than had been done before.

However, this political status is not acceptable to all Puerto Ricans. A considerable sector of the population wishes to see Puerto Rico become a federal state of the Union. The separatist sector seeks total independence from the United States. There are two tendencies within this latter sector. One is more moderate and takes institutional form in the Partido Independentista Puertorriqueño. Both are a minority among the population of the country, but they are an important voice in everyday life. The membership of The United Methodist Church includes voices from these various political tendencies, both among its laity and among its pastors.

A second factor is the role of the missionary. The person of the Methodist missionary during the early years and until the thirties was very controversial. On the one hand, the missionary was credited with coming to the mission field, with all the risks for health and welfare for oneself and for one's family; on the other hand, missionaries had support and privileges that national pastors never received. A simple but eloquent manifestation of this was the existence in the cool mountains near Aibonito of a building that was known as Missionary Rest Home. There hardly ever would a native pastor or lay leader appear, unless it was in order to bring news, run an errand, or serve in the kitchen. Thus the figure of the missionary-superintendent or of the missionary-pastor of that time was that of a benevolent despot. They were lords and masters of a church composed of poor people and a native ministry with little training and ill paid. However, in spite of this the church is grateful to them because they worked with sacrifice and commitment. The least we can say about the missionaries is that they were devoted and helpful, and that their intentions were good. They did not see themselves as instruments of a political and social movement but as messengers of the gospel of Christ.

The first Puerto Rican pastors were converts won by the

preaching of the missionaries. They came from the subcultures of sugarcane, coffee, and tobacco. They were brainy, brilliant, self-taught. They did not mind their own penury, since the vast majority of Puerto Ricans lived in similar circumstances. They paid no heed to the difference in salary and support between themselves and the missionaries. Some were involved in politics, very much so. They even knew about medicine.

The third factor shaping the Puerto Rican Methodist personality is the political and cultural ambivalence that underlies the society in which the church exists. Among Methodists, since the church is connectional in character and is part of the church in the United States, hymnology, ritual, theology, and ecclesiology have been inherited from an Anglo-Saxon tradition. This comes into a cultural context that has five centuries of Hispanic experience. In spite of all the Americanizing process of almost ninety years, the ethnicity of the church remains strong—as is the case in all of Puerto Rican society. The tasks of translating ritual and declarations and for bishops and general leaders of the church and the anguishing struggle to apply structures made for an Anglo society to the particular situation of the island contribute to this ambivalence. Therefore, in the church there have always been voices calling for the acknowledgment of the values proper to Puerto Rican ethnicity. Fortunately, in recent years, with the emphasis the national church has given to ethnic minority churches, Puerto Ricans have achieved many of their goals.

THE SELF-DETERMINATION OF THE CHURCH

As a consequence of the factors just discussed, the need appears within Puerto Rican Methodism to define this ambivalent situation once and for all.

The first step in the recent pilgrimage toward self-sufficiency took place in 1971 when the National Division of the General Board of Global Ministries took the decision, without previous consultation with the Conference of Puerto Rico, to cut the funds being sent to Puerto Rico by $153,000. The superintendent of the church that year was the Reverend Rafael Boissén. In a special session of Annual Conference that took place on August 6, 1971, a report prepared and submitted by Dr. Benjamín Santana was received. This outlined four alternatives: an Autonomous Affiliated Church, a Central Conference, an Episcopal Area, and an Annual Conference come to fruition.

Later, in the regular session of Annual Conference, by motion of the Reverend Rafael Boissén, it was agreed to request the General Conference of the church in the United States to issue an Enabling Act allowing the church in Puerto Rico to become an Affiliated Autonomous Church of The United Methodist Church, when it became advisable. The voices raised in favor of such a move were those of Bishop J. Gordon Howard and Dr. Benjamín Santana. The latter was a delegate from Puerto Rico to the General Conference that took place in Atlanta, Georgia, in April 1972.

Once the Enabling Act was approved—that is to say, once permission was granted—the Conference passed, in May 1974 in Arecibo, a resolution "requesting the status of an Affiliated Autonomous Church as an alternative in the development of self-determination" for the Puerto Rican church.

From that time to the present, some fifteen years, the church has been preparing for that requested status. There were meetings and more meetings, plans and reports presented, definitive dates for autonomy postponed once and again, until in 1980 a group of leaders presented a motion to consider another alternative, that of becoming a Central Conference, as a transitional step toward final autonomy. Such a status would give the church in Puerto Rico all the rights and privileges of autonomy, without its being completely separated from the mother church. This option was defeated in January 1980 by only five votes. However, since the final goal now and in the near future is complete autonomy, both those who support the idea of a Central Conference and those who support total autonomy remain united in their quest for that goal.

OTHER POSITIVE ELEMENTS IN THE CHURCH

Under this heading one can mention the following: the ecumenical character of the church, the charismatic awakening, and the work of women.

From the very appearance of the Methodist Church in the life of Puerto Rico there has been a spirit of openness. There are three very eloquent proofs of interconfessional cooperation. The first has to do with communications. The original newspaper of the Methodist Mission, *El Defensor Cristiano,* was published until 1917, when it merged into what would become known as *Puerto Rico Evangélico,* a bimonthly magazine supported by six of the denominations in Puerto Rico. One of its most outstanding directors was the Reverend Jorge N. Cintrón, a Methodist minister.

The second piece of evidence of the ecumenical spirit of Puerto Rican Methodism is its participation in the Evangelical Union, later known as the Federation of Evangelical Churches, then as the Association of Evangelical Churches of Puerto Rico, and finally as the Evangelical Council of Puerto Rico. Wherever it is necessary to make the voice of the church heard, The United Methodist Church uses the Evangelical Council. It works closely with that organization and supports it financially.

Another expression of ecumenism, and the most important of all, is the strong participation of the church in the Evangelical Seminary of Puerto Rico*, a graduate theological school and member of the Latin-American Association of Theological Schools as well as the Association of Theological Schools. This theological school has produced more than 75 percent of all pastors serving the Methodist Church in Puerto Rico. There are currently more than twenty-five of its graduates serving Methodist Hispanic churches in the United States. Many of its professors have come from the Methodist Church of Puerto Rico, and one of these was president of the seminary.

The Puerto Rican Church is also a member of the Council of Methodist Churches of Latin America (CIEMAL). It also keeps close connections with the Iglesia Evangélica Unida de Puerto

Rico, a denomination that resulted from the missionary work of the former Evangelical United Brethren, a denomination that in the United States joined the Methodist Church in order to form the present United Methodist Church. The ecumenical efforts of these two denominational bodies have taken the shape of joint meetings and of collaboration in the Ryder Memorial Hospital and the Conference Center at Yuquiyú.

The charismatic awakening in The United Methodist Church in Puerto Rico is simply an expression of a broader movement both in the churches in the United States and in the Pentecostal churches of Puerto Rico. This sort of religious awakening is nothing new in Methodism. It was experienced by Methodism in its very beginnings in the eighteenth century. Later in the following century in the United States, itinerant Methodist preachers were moved and inspired by a similar movement. In Puerto Rico the church felt the effects of a partial charismatic awakening in the decade of the 1920s, particularly in events that took place in the town of Comerío. More recently and to a much larger degree, during the decades of the 1970s and 1980s the church has been involved in a charismatic movement. At the beginning this created some uneasiness within the church. Congregations split, and one withdrew permanently from The United Methodist Church. As time has gone by several groups that had withdrawn have become partially reintegrated into the church, and today there is a denomination whose ministers and laity know how to use the positive aspects of the charismatic movement.

The last but not least important factor that should be mentioned is the work of women in the development of the church. From the beginning of the missionary work Dr. Charles W. Drees took steps to have deaconesses and women teachers sent from the United States to serve in the schools that were being organized in San Juan, Puerta de Tierra, Ponce, Arecibo, Guayama, and Aibonito. As some of these primary schools were closed, the only one remaining was Robinson School in Santurce, which was originally a home for orphan girls.

Women have also been very active in the ministry of the church.

At the beginning they helped in visitation, as assistants to pastors, and as directors of Christian education. Now many are pastors. Among the early women missionaries the first is remembered with love. She was Sara P. White, who worked only two years, from 1900 to 1902. Then came Alice McKinley and Mrs. J. C. Murray, superintendent of the Robinson Home for Orphans; Bernice Huff, director of kindergartens; Estella Howard and Helen Aldrich, both superintendents of Robinson. Among the first Puerto Ricans women leaders one must mention Mercedes Núñez, Fulgencia Constantino, and Carmen Velázquez. From a later time the church remembers deaconesses Doris Armes and Ilo Stewart. Julia Torres Fernández and Dolores Lebrón Andújar worked in the active pastorate of the church. In more recent times the church in Puerto Rico has had a greater number of women pastors. There are currently eleven serving churches, and the superintendent is a woman, the Reverend Myriam Visot.

The women's organization in the Annual Conference, which was formerly known as the Women's Society of Christian Service, is now known as United Methodist Women of Puerto Rico. Its first president was Antonia M. Pereles. Among those who have presided over that organization, Julia Torres, Eulalia G. de Cruz, Angélica C. Sánchez, Miguelina Rosa Viruet, and Olga Sáez are most remembered. The present president is Abigail Williams. Two women are particularly noteworthy for their work in founding the Conference Center in Guardarraya: Roselia C. de Rico and Olga M. Sáez.

Another positive element is the missionary consciousness that Puerto Rican Methodism has always had. The first signs of this spirit were seen in 1919, when the church in Puerto Rico responded to a request that it send Puerto Rican missionaries to Santo Domingo. Manuel Andújar was sent by Bishop Franklin E. Hamilton to visit that neighboring republic. As a result of that visit, arrangements were made to send Puerto Rican missionaries. Since this was an interdenominational effort, the first missionaries went from other churches, but in 1923 the Reverend José Espada Marrero was sent, and he was followed by others, such as the Reverend Alfredo Rivera, the Reverend Apolinario Cruz

Sánchez, the Reverend Domingo Marrero, and the Reverend José Seguí. The work of this group of five missionaries covers a period of twenty-four years during which the church in Puerto Rico sent and supported Puerto Rican missionaries in the Evangelical Dominican Church. The sending of missionaries to the Dominican Republic ceased when Dominican candidates to the ministry began taking their place. These were trained at the Evangelical Seminary of Puerto Rico and later at the Theological Seminary in Matanzas, Cuba.

More recently, in 1980, the Puerto Rico Annual Conference sent the Reverend Héctor Soto Vélez as a missionary to Argentina. Furthermore, since 1977 the Conference has been sending pastors to work in the United States. There are more than twenty-five of these. This is Puerto Rico's way of expressing its gratitude to the mother church. At one time that church sent us missionaries, but it is now Puerto Rico that sends them to the mother church so that it may continue its work among the growing Hispanic population of that country. Likewise, several Puerto Rican pastors have served in key positions in the general agencies of the church in the United States.

The United Methodist Church of Puerto Rico, as it approaches the twenty-first century, has clearly defined goals and knows where it is going. Its goal is complete autonomy, so that then, jointly with all the other Methodist churches of the world, it may be able to do its part as a member of the body of Christ. In a world in crisis such as ours, the church must examine and evaluate itself and put all its resources at the service of Jesus Christ, Lord of the church and of the world.

Editor's note: The Reverend Gildo Sánchez, the author of this chapter) was president of the seminary.

8

THE NEXT FIVE
HUNDRED YEARS

Justo L. González

Although we usually think of history in terms of the past,
history is also about the future. As we study our past, we do so the
better to understand our present, and to make decisions about the
future. Thus the past history whose survey we have completed
would be incomplete without some reflections on our present
situation, and the future from which God is calling us.

As this book goes to press, we are approaching the fifth
centennial of the so-called discovery of America. In 1992 the first
five centuries of a tragic and glorious history will come to an end,
and Hispanic Americans will move into the sixth century of our
existence as the mixed race that we are. What will be the agenda of
Hispanic United Methodists in that sixth century of our existence?
That is the issue to which we must turn as we complete our rapid
survey of Hispanic United Methodist history.

As we look at that agenda, it is clear that its foremost item will
be unity. The first reflection arising from the survey we have just
completed is that we are not as fragmented as that survey may have
implied. For reasons both practical and historical, it was decided
to divide our survey by jurisdictions, with one chapter for each of
the five jurisdictions of The United Methodist Church, plus a
separate chapter for our history in Puerto Rico. It is true that
Hispanic Methodism has had several centers in the United States:
one in the West and Southwest, with connections mostly with
Mexico; one in the Northeast, with connections mostly with

Puerto Rico; and one in the Southeast, with connections mostly with Cuba. The differences arising from these various traditions and connections are very real to this day, and therefore one option would have been to outline our history in terms of those three foci and connections. Yet it is also true that the division of the entire denomination into jurisdictions has influenced the lives of Hispanic Methodists in a number of ways, and for that reason it was decided to use that division as the basis for our outline.

At the same time, those divisions are not the entire picture. Indeed, as one surveys the more recent history of Hispanic Methodism, it is clear that the one outstanding feature of that history is our growth toward ever-greater unity. This has been fostered by the movement of laity across Conference and jurisdictional lines; by national meetings of women, many of whom have taken the lead in this quest for unity; and by a series of publications that have opened the way toward greater commonality.

Among the publications that have promoted our unity, *Lecciones cristianas* is the one with the longest history of publication. It was started by the Board of Education of the Methodist Church in 1957, originally as a translation from English. In the 1960s this quarterly magazine for adult Sunday school classes began publishing lessons originally written in Spanish, most of them by Hispanic leaders in the Methodist Church. Its editors through the years have been Rhoda Edmeston, Arnold Sherman, Ariel Zambrano, Edgar and Donna Moros, and Carmen Gaud. Until 1984 it was the only regular publication in Spanish of the United Methodist Publishing House. In 1986 it was expanded to include a separate publication for teachers. The impact of *Lecciones cristianas* has been widespread, for it is used not only by the vast majority of Hispanic United Methodist congregations but also by a number of other denominations. By special arrangement, the American Baptist Convention issues its own edition of the magazine, with the same lessons as The United Methodist Church but with a different title. This magazine, whose impact on our theology has been undeniable, merits special historical study and research, for it constitutes a record of the development of Hispanic hermeneutics and theology as yet untapped by our historians.

Another publication that has had significant impact on the Hispanic United Methodist community is *El intérprete*. The roots of this publication reach far back to a periodical that was published in Cuba, *El evangelista cubano*. It began as an adaptation of *The Methodist Story*, under the title *Acción metodista*, in 1958. After a period of inactivity it was reorganized under the leadership of Dr. Jorge N. Cintrón, a distinguished pastor, educator, and journalist in Puerto Rico. He directed the magazine from 1965 to 1971, and when he left this responsibility the magazine ceased publication once more. It was then reorganized under a national board and recommenced publication in 1973. Since that time it has continued regular publication, first under the leadership of the Reverend Finees Flores and then of Ms. Edith Lafontaine. As a magazine dealing mostly with programmatic issues, it has given Hispanic United Methodists a greater sense of unity in their programs and has also served as a forum where ideas are shared and discussed.

In 1973 the *Himnario Metodista* was published by the United Methodist Publishing House. It was a project of the Río Grande Conference, which in 1955 had published its own hymnal. This new book was produced under the leadership of Dr. Alfredo Náñez. Although originally a project of the Río Grande Conference, it soon attained widespread circulation among Hispanic United Methodists in other Conferences. Its impact has been of enormous significance, for the use of the same hymns and similar liturgies has bound Hispanic Methodists more than any other single factor. Also, the *Himnario Metodista* has played an important role in our self-esteem and self-expression, for it includes a number of hymns that have become classics in our churches, many of which were written by the early leaders whose names appear in other chapters of this book.

Continuing along the same lines, the Board of Discipleship has published two smaller songbooks: *Celebremos* and *Celebremos II*. These contain almost exclusively hymnody that is Hispanic both in origin and in flavor. The contrast between *Celebremos,* published in 1979, and *Celebremos II,* published in 1983, is striking and serves to illustrate the direction in which Hispanic United Methodism is moving. The second songbook, which has been very well received and is widely used in our churches, is remarkable in its use of various Hispanic musical traditions, but also in its theology, which is a clear call to mission and to presence in the world, in contrast with many of the songs in the first book, which tended to be more individualistic. Also, *Celebremos II* includes more hymnody from Latin America, thus contributing to the contacts with that part of the body of Christ that are so important for Hispanics in the United States.

More recently, under the auspices of the Mexican-American Program of Perkins School of Theology, and with the support of the United Methodist Publishing House, a journal of theology from a Hispanic perspective, *Apuntes,* has been widely received and discussed, not only among United Methodists but also by members of a wide variety of denominations.

The contact fostered by all these publications has found more concrete expression in a number of national and regional events that have been landmarks in our path toward greater unity. Probably the most important of these was the founding of the Hispanic caucus, MARCHA. Once again, the very birth of MARCHA illustrates the importance that ecumenical contacts have had for Hispanic United Methodists. It was at a meeting of the Council on Hispanic American Ministries (COHAM) in San Antonio that the United Methodist delegates decided that the time had come for a Hispanic caucus within their own denomination. This was organized a year later, in 1971, at El Paso. Its first president was the Reverend Elías Galván, later to be elected the first Hispanic bishop in The United Methodist Church (or its predecessor churches). At General Conference the following year, many of the dreams and frustrations of Hispanic United Methodists were expressed in the cry, "Viva MARCHA!" Since that time MARCHA has played an important role in the struggles of Hispanics to find the necessary support and room for their mission, as well as in the more general struggle along similar lines of all the ethnic minority groups in the denomination. For

155

instance, MARCHA joined with other minority caucuses in advocating for the extension of the missional priority on the Ethnic Minority Local Church by the General Conference of 1984, when the General Council on Ministries opposed it.

Along with the work of MARCHA, a number of meetings and events have fostered our unity. Perhaps the most significant of these was the National Hispanic Consultation, meeting in Los Angeles in 1979, which for the first time gave us a sense of the power and enthusiasm of the Hispanic United Methodist constituency.

In short, as we approach the sixth century of Hispanic American history, unity is the primary focus of our agenda.

This, however, is not the totality of our agenda. The very date 1992 forces us into a process of historical analysis and self-understanding. As was said in our first chapter, the history that began in 1492 is neither pretty nor pure. Yet it is out of that history that we have emerged, and while we deeply deplore the injustices that are part of it, we must also find ways to celebrate our own existence and identity as part of its result. It may be difficult for others to see this, for the dominant view of history in our society—as in any society—is one that seeks to justify the existing status quo by showing that it is the result of high ideals and glorious deeds. That is the way those in power tend to write the official history of a nation, a civilization, or a church.

We, however, must begin to develop a different view of history, a realistic one in which there are no good guys and bad guys, no white hats and black hats, but frail and sinful human beings struggling in quest of their own identities and destinies, often at the expense of others. As we look at our own history with honesty, we will come to what could be called a non-innocent view of history, one that no longer asks merely who was right but rather what were the forces—social, economic, religious—at play in a given conflict, and how they helped determine the outcome. To this must be added, for those of us who ask this question from a perspective of faith, two further questions: How do we discern God's will in such a history without heroes or saints? How do we discern that will in our own days, when a similar history is

156

unfolding? While such a non-innocent view of history will be the result of our reflection on our history as Hispanics, one could also argue that this is part of the biblical understanding and description of history, and that therefore as we study our history from this painful perspective, we shall also be helping the entire church clarify its understanding of the biblical message.

In any case, one of the most significant events in our recent history is that we have begun to reflect critically on our own history. While the preceding chapters have attempted above all to record the events as they are remembered by those who lived through them and as they can be reconstructed from contemporary records, there is a further task that must now be undertaken, and that has already begun. That is the task of reinterpreting our history, both as United Methodists and as Hispanics, from this perspective of a non-innocent view of history. What this means first of all is that we must come to grips, as Hispanics, with the skeletons in our historical closet. This is not difficult, since the dominant culture and its own writing of history are quite willing to point out such skeletons. Yet we must remember and acknowledge that we are the children of Cortez and La Malinche, of conqueror and conquered, of slave and master. This is a task that has been undertaken by many of the leading figures in Hispanic thought, and that we must appropriate not only as individuals but also as a people, in order to come to grips with the complexities of our own identities.

Then we must make a difficult and unwelcome but necessary contribution to the dominant culture, correcting its reading of history, so that it too can see that its own history is non-innocent and thus be ready to do justice today. Indeed, one of the reasons why the reading of history as a clash between the good and the bad is so popular is that it implies that since the good won, and the present order is the result of that history, the present order must be good, and there is little need to change it. An apparently naive and innocent reading of history results in very guilty acts of injustice today.

Finally, we must begin to apply this methodology to our own reading and writing of Hispanic United Methodist history. There too the motives were mixed. There too there were economic, social, and political forces at work, and many of those who thought they were the main actors were not aware of the role that such forces played. Then, by such writing of history, we shall be able to make our contribution to the present task of the church—which is also its perennial task—of seeking out what it means to be faithful in the making of today's history.

This rereading of history has begun at a number of places. The most significant is probably the series of symposia that are taking place under the auspices of the Mexican-American Program of Perkins School of Theology. These symposia, sharing the general title of "*Redescubrimiento*" and built around the theme of the fifth centennial of 1492, seek to rediscover both our history and our own identity in the light of that history, in order then to explore what may be our mission today. The first of the series, held in 1987, brought together Hispanic leaders from all parts of the country and from Puerto Rico, as well as from several different denominations. The second symposium, held in 1990, sought to elicit greater and more active participation from the grass roots of the Hispanic community.

It is clear that in all this Hispanic United Methodists are moving beyond the bounds of their own denomination. This is a further item in our agenda. The denominational structures and divisions of our society generally reflect the structures and divisions of the dominant culture and do not always help or support the needs of minorities. Thus it is imperative for Hispanic United Methodists to establish closer links beyond the confines of The United Methodist Church. This is currently being done at three levels: First, there is much more direct contact between Hispanics in the United States and their sisters and brothers in Latin America. Second, there is much greater contact across ecumenical lines. Third, there is an increasing spirit of collaboration and of a common struggle joining Hispanics to other minorities. A current example of this is the Roundtable of Ethnic Theologians, under the auspices of the Division of Ordained Ministry of the Board of Higher Education and Ministry. This Roundtable has brought together ethnic minority United Methodist theologians around a common agenda. Significantly, part of that agenda focuses on the year 1992, seeking to make certain that on this occasion the real meeting and understanding that did not take place five hundred years ago begins to take place. Many of us are convinced that the more such contacts are cultivated and strengthened, the more will the Reign of God be served.

The General Conference of 1988 has finally come to grips with one of the main shortcomings of the Hispanic work both of The United Methodist Church and of the denominations that have come together to form it: the lack of a total strategy for Hispanic work, one conceived and shaped by Hispanics. Upon petition from MARCHA, General Conference ordered that a special committee be formed "to develop a comprehensive national plan for Hispanic Ministries for the United Methodist Church," and that this plan be presented to the 1992 General Conference.

As this committee brings its report, it is to be expected that much of what it will recommend will require significant changes and adaptations, not only on matters of strategy but also on policy and structure. For United Methodist Hispanics wondering about our next five hundred years, the manner in which the denomination at large responds to the recommendations of that committee will be an indication of what the sixth century of our history as Hispanics will bring. It is our prayer that it will bring greater faithfulness, and a missionary outreach that really reaches the masses of our population, so that it will truly come to pass that we shall all hear the gospel "each in our own tongue."

CHRONOLOGY

1492	Arrival of first Spaniards in the Western Hemisphere
1508–11	Conquest of Puerto Rico
1511–15	Conquest of Cuba
1521	Ponce de León in Florida; siege and fall of Tenochtitlan (Mexico City)
1540–43	Various Spanish expeditions explore the Pacific coast to Oregon and reach the Grand Canyon.
1541	De Soto reaches the Mississippi.
1565	Founding of Saint Augustine, Florida
1610	Founding of Santa Fe, New Mexico
1620	Mayflower Pilgrims
1720–22	Spanish occupy Texas.
1736	John Wesley begins to study Spanish.
1738	Aldersgate
1769	Founding of San Diego, California
1776	Founding of San Francisco, California
1781	Founding of Los Angeles, California
1834	David Ayers distributes Bibles in Spanish in South Texas.
1836	Texas declares its independence from Mexico.
1842	Birth of Alejo Hernández
1848	Treaty of Guadalupe-Hidalgo; United States takes over half of Mexico's territory.

1849–50	First large influx of Cubans into Florida
1853	Benigno Cárdenas preaches in Spanish in Santa Fe.
1861–65	U.S. Civil War
1862	French invade Mexico.
1868–78	Cuban Ten Years' War for independence against Spain; Cuban migration to Florida accelerates.
1869	Thomas Harwood reopens New Mexico mission for Methodist Episcopal Church.
1871	Alejo Hernández is ordained deacon.
1872	Methodist Episcopal Church, South, begins work in Mexico.
1873	Hernández organizes first congregation in Mexico City and is ordained elder. José Vanduzer is appointed to serve Cubans in Key West, Florida.
1875	Death of Alejo Hernández in Corpus Christi, Texas; death of José Vanduzer in Key West
1877	First Hispanic church building in Key West is built.
1880	Antonio Díaz begins work in Los Angeles.
1881	Santiago Tafolla is appointed first Mexican presiding elder.
1885	New Mexico Spanish Mission is organized. Mexican Border Conference is organized.
1886	Martínez-Ybor moves tobacco factory to Tampa, Florida, from Key West.
1888	Primitivo Rodríguez begins translating and editing resources in Spanish for Methodist Episcopal Church (in Nashville, Tennessee).
1889	Enrique Someillán is first Cuban pastor in Key West.
1891	Santiago H. Limbs begins work in Los Angeles.
1892	First Methodist Church of Tampa begins Hispanic work.
1894	Someillán goes to Tampa. More churches and institutions founded in Tampa.
1896	Manuel Deulofeu is second Cuban pastor in Key West.
1898	Sinking of the *Maine*; Spanish-American War; United States sovereignty over Puerto Rico and Cuba

1899 Exploratory visits to Puerto Rico by Leonard and Ninde

1900 C. W. Drees arrives at Puerto Rico. First service is celebrated. First congregations are organized. Washington Institute and McKinley Free School are founded.

1902 Porto Rico Mission is organized. Juan Vázquez is first Puerto Rican to be licenced as local preacher.

1903 Magazine *El Defensor Cristiano* is founded in Puerto Rico. Director is the Reverend Manuel Andújar.

1904 B. S. Haywood succeeds Drees as superintendent.

1907 New Mexico Mission is discontinued as separate unit.

1908 Methodist Episcopal Church, South, opens Mary J. Platt School for "Spanish girls" in Tucson.

1909 The Spanish-American School for boys opens.

1910 Beginning of Mexican Revolution

1913 Lydia Patterson Institute is founded at El Paso, Texas. Missionary Conference of Puerto Rico is organized.

1914 The mission of Methodist Episcopal Church, South, in Mexico and Texas is separated into two units. The Texas Mexican Mission is organized at Austin, Texas. The Latin District of the Florida Conference is founded.

1915 A second Hispanic church is organized in Key West.

1917 Pancho Villa raids Columbus, New Mexico. United States enters World War I. *El defensor cristiano* and other denominational publications merge into *Puerto Rico evangélico*.

1911 Vernon L. McCombs is named Superintendent of Spanish Work for the Southern California Annual Conference, a position he holds until 1946.

1914 General Conference of Methodist Episcopal Church, South, organizes the Pacific Mexican Mission.

1915 Plaza Community Center is organized in Los Angeles.

1919	Bible Institute in Hatillo, Puerto Rico, merges with others to found Evangelical Seminary of Puerto Rico.
1920	Wesleyan Institute is founded in San Antonio, Texas. Methodist Episcopal Church establishes Latin American Mission for Western Arizona and California.
1926	Foundation of first Hispanic church in Northern Illinois Conference
1929	Death of Andújar, a missionary in Puerto Rico for twenty-nine years and superintendent for eighteen. He is succeeded by B. R. Campbell.
1929-39	The Great Depression. Five hundred thousand Mexicans are deported.
1930	Texas Mexican Mission becomes Texas Mexican Conference.
1932	Work declines in Key West. Trinity Methodist Church in Miami begins Hispanic work.
1936	Last missionary employed by Mission Board to serve Hispanic area of present Río Grande Conference
1939	Three branches of Methodism unite at Kansas City, Missouri. Southwest Mexican Conference is organized, bringing together the Spanish-speaking churches in New Mexico and Texas. Latin District of Florida is dissolved. World War II begins.
1941	U.S. enters World War II. Provisional Annual Conference of Puerto Rico is organized. Latin American Provisional Conference is organized.
1942	Bracero program begins. United Brethren begin Hispanic work in Tampa.
1946	Luis P. Tirre is first Latino superintendent in California.
1948	Southwest Mexican Conference becomes Río Grande Conference. Reorganization of mission in Miami as Spanish-American Methodist Church and Latin Center.

1949	Tomás Rico Soltero is first Puerto Rican superintendent, a position he holds until his death in 1971.
1955	Rio Grande Conference rejects merger recommendations. First *Hymnario Metodista* is published.
1956	Dissolution of Latin American Provisional Conference in California
1959	Cuban Revolution; Cuban migration to Miami, Florida
1960	Foundation of first Hispanic church in Cleveland, Ohio
1961	Break of relations between United States and Cuba. Missionaries recalled. Cuban pastors follow. Work in Tamiami is begun by H. R. Carrazana. Work at six more sites is begun shortly thereafter. Last Hispanic church in Tampa is closed by Annual Conference.
1965	Grape workers strike in Delano, California. Vietnam war escalates. National Division agrees to place administration of funds in hands of Río Grande Conference Board of Missions. J. Lloyd Knox is appointed to coordinate Hispanic work in Florida. Spanish-American Church and Latin Center are expropriated.
1966	Texas Valley Farmworkers strike and march to Austin.
1967	Río Grande Conference votes to continue as separate unit. Puerto Rico Annual Conference is organized.
1968	Evangelical United Brethren and Methodist Church merge. Central Jurisdiction is eliminated. LAMAG is organized in California (Elías Galván, president).
1970	Steering Committee for MARCHA is organized in San Antonio. First Hispanic church in Detroit is founded.
1972	General Conference passes Enabling Act, authorizing prospective autonomy for church in Puerto Rico.
1973	A committee of four Hispanic pastors is set up to coordinate work in Florida.

1974   Puerto Rico Annual Conference votes for affiliated autonomy.

1975   Gildo Sánchez is appointed superintendent of Puerto Rico Annual Conference. Work in Florida is reorganized under Hispanic Committee on Ministries. First Consultation on Hispanic Strategy in Florida meets.

1979   Foundation of a Hispanic church in Kenosha, Wisconsin.

1980   Foundation of first Hispanic churches in Iowa and St. Paul, Minnesota

1981   Luis F. Sotomayor is superintendent of Puerto Rico. First Hispanic church in Indianapolis, Indiana, is founded.

1982   Foundation of first Hispanic church in Milwaukee, Wisconsin

1985   Myriam Visot is first woman superintendent of Puerto Rico.

1986   Second Consultation on Hispanic Strategy in Florida meets.

1988   Appointment of first woman bishop of Puerto Rico

BIBLIOGRAPHY

BOOKS AND ARTICLES

Brooks, W., ed. *From Saddlebags to Satellites: A History of Florida Methodism*. Florida Annual Conference, 1969.

Browne, Jefferson B. *Key West: The Old and the New*. Gainesville, Fla.: University of Florida Press, 1973.

Castellanos, Gerardo. *Motivos de Cayo Hueso*. La Habana: Ucar, García y cia., 1935.

Cepeda, Rafael, ed. *La herencia misionera en Cuba: Consulta de las iglesias protestantes realizada en Matanzas, Cuba, en 1984*. San José, Costa Rica: DEI, 1986.

Christian Work in Latin America. New York, Missionary Education Movement, 1917.

Cox, Ezra M. "Latin American Provisional Conference." In *Annual Report of the Division of Home Missions and Church Extension of the Board of Missions and Church Extension of the Methodist Church*. New York: Board of Missions and Church Extension of The United Methodist Church, 1947, pp. 107-9.

Crahan, Margaret E. *Religious Penetration and Nationalism in Cuba: U.S. Methodist Activities 1898–1958*. Revista Review Interamericana. San Germán, Puerto Rico: Interamerican University of Puerto Rico, 1978.

Davis, J. Merle. *The Church in Puerto Rico's Dilemma: A Study of the Economic and Social Basis of the Evangelical Church in Puerto Rico.* New York: International Missionary Council, 1942.

Davis, J. Merle. *The Cuban Church in a Sugar Economy.* New York: International Missionary Council, 1942.

Díaz Acosta, Juan. *Historia de la Iglesia Evangélica Unida de Puerto Rico. Obra evangélica para el cincuentenario en Puerto Rico: 1899–1949.* San Juan, Puerto Rico: Iglesia Evangélica Unida de Puerto Rico, 1949.

Estenger, Rafael. *Sincera historia de Cuba: 1492–1973.* Medellín: Bedout, 1974.

Florida State Library Board. *Guide to Supplementary Vital Statistics from Church Records in Florida.* Tallahassee, Fla.: Florida State Library Board, 1942.

Foner, Philip S. *La guerra hispano-cubano-americana y el nacimiento del imperialismo norteamericano.* Madrid: Akal, 1975.

Ford Foundation. *Los hispanos: problemas y oportunidades.* New York: Ford Foundation, 1984.

Fox, Geoffrey E. *Working-class Emigres from Cuba.* Palo Alto, Calif.: R. & E. Research Associates, 1979.

González, Justo L. *The Development of Christianity in the Latin Caribbean.* Grand Rapids, Mich.: Eerdmans, 1969.

———. *The Theological Education of Hispanics.* New York: The Fund for Theological Education, 1988.

Harwood, Thomas. *History of the New Mexico, Spanish and English Missions.* Albuquerque, N. Mex.: El Abogado Press, 1908.

Haselden, Kyle. *Death of a Myth: New Locus for Spanish American Faith.* New York: Friendship, 1964.

Horton, H. G. *Beginnings of the Mexican Work.* Austin, Tex.: The Texas Historical Society, 1920.

Inventory of the Records of the Cuban Consulate from 1886 to 1961. Austin, Tex.: The University of Texas at Austin, 1983. Microfilm.

Isern, José J. *Gobernadores cubanos de la Florida.* N.p., n.d.

Isern, José J. *Pioneros cubanos en U.S.A., 1575–1898.* Key West, Fla.: Cenit Printing, Club San Carlos, 1971.

Jervey, Edward Drewry. *The History of Methodism in Southern California-Arizona.* Nashville: Parthenon Press, 1960.

Kellog, Harriet S. *Life of Mrs. Emily J. Harwood.* Albuquerque, N. Mex.: El Abogado Press, 1903.

Lucas, Isidro. *The Browning of America: The Hispanic Revolution in the American Church.* Chicago: Fides/Claretian, 1981.

Ludwig, E., and Santibáñez, James, eds. *The Chicanos: Mexican American Voices.* Baltimore: Penguin Books, 1971.

Mead, Frank S. *On Our Own Doorstep.* New York: Friendship Press, 1948.

Moore, Donald T. *Puerto Rico Para Cristo: A History of the Progress of the Evangelical Missions in the Island of Puerto Rico.* Cuernavaca: Centro Intercultural de Documentación, 1969.

Muñoz, Esaú P. *Memorias de Esaú P. Muñoz: Historias de fe y amor al principio del evangelio en el norte de México.* México: Casa Unida de Publicaciones, S.A., 1987.

Nail, Olin W. *The First One Hundred Years: 1858–1959, The Southwest Texas Conference of the Methodist Church.* Austin, Tex.: Southwest Texas Conference, 1958.

Náñez, Alfredo. *Historia de la Conferencia de Río Grande de la Iglesia Metodista Unida.* Dallas: Bridwell Library of Southern Methodist University, 1981. (There is also an English edition, from the same publisher and date.)

Neblett, Sterling Augustus. *Historia de la Iglesia Metodista en Cuba.* Buenos Aires: El Evangelista Cubano, 1973.

Neblett, Sterling Augustus. *Methodism in Cuba: The First Thirteen Years.* Macon, Ga.: Wesleyan College, 1966.

Pérez, Carlos. *Setenta años de labor de la Iglesia Metodista en Cuba: 1898–1968.* Miami, 1983.

Ramos, Marcos A. *Panorama del Protestantismo en Cuba.* Miami: Caribe, 1986.

Rodríguez, Daniel R. *La primera evangelización norteamericana en Puerto Rico, 1898–1930.* México: Ediciones Borinquen, 1986.

Sáenz, Michael. *Economic Aspects of Church Development in Puerto Rico: A Study of the Financial Policies and Procedures of the Major Protestant Church Groups in Puerto Rico from 1898 to 1957.* Ann Arbor, Mich.: University Microfilm, 1962.

Sánchez, Gildo. *Un jirón de historia metodista.* San Juan, Puerto Rico, 1981.

Shope, John M. *Los puertorriqueños y la Biblia*. San Germán, Puerto Rico: Center for Research in Cultural Change, 1962.

Sprinkle, Henry C. *Spanish Doorways: American Methodism and the Evangelical Mission among Spanish-Speaking Neighbors*. New York: World Outlook Press, 1964.

Thrift, Charles T., Jr. *The Trail of the Florida Circuit Rider: An Introduction to the Rise of Methodism in Middle and East Florida*. Lakeland, Fla.: Florida Southern College Press, 1944.

Tirre, L. P. "A Flying Trip to the Stations." In *Annual Report of the Division of Home Missions and Church Extension of the Board of Missions and Church Extension of the Methodist Church*. New York: Board of Missions and Church Extension of The United Methodist Church, 1947, pp. 109-12.

Toledo, Reinaldo, ed. *Centenario de la obra metodista hispana en Cayo Hueso: 1874–1974*. Key West, Fla.: Iglesia Metodista Unida El Salvador, 1974.

Westfall, L. Glenn., *Key West: Cigar City U.S.A.* Key West, Fla.: The Historic Key West Preservation Board, 1984.

Whyman, Henry C. *The History of Ethnic Ministries in the New York Conference, The United Methodist Church*. New York: The New York Conference Bicentennial Committee, 1984.

MANUSCRIPTS AND DISSERTATIONS

Arturet, Antonio. "Desarrollo histórico de la Iglesia Evangélica Unida de Puerto Rico." B.D. thesis, Seminario Evangélico de Puerto Rico, 1965.

Cabrera Leiva, Guillermo. "El protestantismo norteamericano en las Antillas españolas." M.A. thesis, University of Miami, 1951.

Fernández, José Moreno. "The History and Prospects of Hispanic Methodism in the Southern California-Arizona Conference of the United Methodist Church." Ph.D. dissertation, Claremont School of Theology, 1973.

Zambrano, Ariel. "Content and Context of Evangelization: An Hispanic Perspective." D.Min. dissertation, Claremont School of Theology, 1986.

PERIODICALS

There are a number of periodicals in which one finds numerous articles on the history of Hispanic Methodism:

Acción Metodista
Apuntes
California Christian Advocate
Daily Christian Advocate
El defensor cristiano
El evangelista cubano
El evangelista mexicano
El heraldo cristiano
El intérprete
El mensajero metodista
La cadena de oro
Lecciones cristianas
Puerto Rico Evangélico
Revista Trimestral
Texas Christian Advocate

OTHER RESOURCES

The authors of the various chapters have also made use of archival material, some of it in local churches and some in a number of depositories. The depositories most often used were the collections at the Evangelical Seminary of Puerto Rico, Perkins School of Theology, and Claremont School of Theology.

INDEX

Compiled by
Edward C. Zaragoza
Methodist Assistant for Ethnic History
General Commission on Archives and History

171

Index

172

Index

Index

Index

Index